Routledge Revivals

The Individual and the Community

First published in 1922, *The Individual and the Community* is a simple statement of the principles which underlie human activities, and condition the combined efforts of two or more individuals: with a comparison of human and animal communities, a distinction between community and State, and a forecast of communal evolution. It is a handbook of human co-existence. This book will be of interest to students of philosophy.

The Individual and the Community

R. E. Roper

First published in 1922
By George Allen & Unwin Ltd.

This edition first published in 2024 by Routledge
4 Park Square, Milton Park, Abingdon, Oxon, OX14 4RN

and by Routledge
605 Third Avenue, New York, NY 10017

Routledge is an imprint of the Taylor & Francis Group, an informa business

© George Allen & Unwin, 1922

All rights reserved. No part of this book may be reprinted or reproduced or utilised in any form or by any electronic, mechanical, or other means, now known or hereafter invented, including photocopying and recording, or in any information storage or retrieval system, without permission in writing from the publishers.

Publisher's Note
The publisher has gone to great lengths to ensure the quality of this reprint but points out that some imperfections in the original copies may be apparent.

Disclaimer
The publisher has made every effort to trace copyright holders and welcomes correspondence from those they have been unable to contact.

A Library of Congress record exists under LCCN: 23000973

ISBN: 978-1-032-76955-4 (hbk)
ISBN: 978-1-003-48057-0 (ebk)
ISBN: 978-1-032-76957-8 (pbk)

Book DOI 10.4324/9781003480570

THE INDIVIDUAL &
THE COMMUNITY

BY

R. E. ROPER, M.A., M.Ed.

LONDON: GEORGE ALLEN & UNWIN LTD.
RUSKIN HOUSE, 40 MUSEUM STREET, W.C.1

First published in 1922

(All rights reserved)

PREFACE

LOOKING back across the chasm which has been torn open between us and our recent past, we see the ruins of that Western European civilisation which once we believed so permanent. Behind them in perspective are ranged other ruins, of Rome, of Greece, Egypt, Asia,—mighty organisations of trade and empire whose fragments crowd our museums. Behind these again are still other ruins, hidden under sand or in forests, beneath the tumbled rocks of earthquake or avalanche, or under the smooth creeping sea. Yet the plan of their building remains in our minds as a heritage of failure, that plan which never brought success but only power, dominion and glory. And to-day the statesmen of the world and their anxious followers grabble like frenzied ants among the ruins of memory, belief and hope, seizing now this now that, carrying, dragging and dropping it afresh in their desperate struggle of reconstruction.

Meanwhile the peoples of the earth, distrustful and disillusioned, set about their daily toil—where such is to be found, driven by a force more natural and more powerful than the laws of states, as urgent as the need of food—the necessity of creative work.

At Versailles, at Spa, Lympne, Washington or

San Remo, each in their different way typical of the power of money, the representatives of wealth have striven to reincarnate the spirit of past empire according to the ancient plan, forgetful or careless of the ruin it has always brought. Students of history and sociology who back their efforts, themselves steeped in the study of past dominion, model their theoretical community of the future upon the lines of those bygone groupings whose fragments litter the world from Babylon to Mexico. Yet though they patch and cobble, and buttress their new-old leagues with every sanction known to man, their work will crumble in their hands.

All that is vital in human community, all that ever built the shrivelled honeycombs of the past, the force which sweeps statesmen and politicians here and there like corks upon a wave, may be found among men and women and children as they lead their daily lives. Two persons meeting in a street, a blacksmith in a forge, children at play, a chance-met group of people round a fallen horse, these and such as these are the material of sociology and statesmanship. In them may be seen at work the laws which govern human nature : from them and their like may be deduced the conditions favourable to its further evolution. Here is no affair of high policy or secret diplomacy, no hidden mystery, no jealously-guarded preserve of experts, but a plain issue of human life, within the grasp of and affecting all.

The artificial nature of the frontiers which separate states to-day is clear to anyone who has passed Modane or Delle, or other homes of tragic comedy and discomfort. Lines slashed across a plain, or cross-gartering an artery of traffic with more than Malvolio's absurdity, shutting off rivers from their mouths and factories from their raw material, were futile enough in the past. To begin now to cut up Europe into a new jig-saw puzzle, even though the design be arranged amidst the gilt and mirrors of former kings of France, cannot be regarded as a serious contribution to life by the men and women who have the world's work to do. We need something more real and more practical: these old men's games get in our way. It is we who have to live in the communities of the earth and to change them to our needs: we will make them for ourselves. The empires of the past have brought us death. Our towns to-day are hopelessly congested, our country districts underpopulated. We sweat and starve for a miserable pittance and fight with one another for a chance to work. To vast numbers of people our vaunted civilisation is a mockery and a farce. Let us experiment: let us make something new. Nothing we invent can be much worse than what we have, and at least it will be our own to change and improve. We can no longer afford to delegate our activities if we hope to live secure: we dare not run the risk of further ruin.

The material for research is in our reach. All that we need is some indication of the lines which our enquiry may best follow: the rest we can do for ourselves. What is a community, what is an individual human being, what are the natural laws which condition our activities and our coexistence, these we must first discover. For the rest we may rely not on the patent medicines of the politician, not even on the authority of the most expert professor, but on the common sense of the ordinary man and woman and child. And this we can do with the greater hope, because it is just this common sense which is the present sum of past experience: it is this which has enabled human evolution to proceed in spite of empires and in the face of tradition. It is this which causes humanity at large to revolt against the senseless stupidity and wastefulness of war. It is the basis of that trust and confidence upon which all communal effort must depend. It is ahead of law, and rules and regulations, for these are always of the past, whereas common sense lives in the present and calculates upon the future. Call it instinctive, inherited or acquired, it is in essentials the application of past experience to future needs.

Nowhere are words more vaguely and varyingly used than in connection with the activities of the human mind: we are faced at the outset of the enquiry with the need of a dictionary of terms. For practical purposes it does not matter with what meaning a word is used, so long as the meaning is clearly and definitely stated. If one person says twice two makes four, and another that it makes sixteen, it is as well to make sure of the value intended so as to be able to allow for the factor of error and make the necessary calculations. Far more disastrous mistakes may be made if one is vague as to the meaning given to such words as mind, brain, instinct, nation, community and the like. I have

PREFACE

therefore included a list of definitions of such words, giving the sense in which they are used in this book. It will thus be more easy to translate them into the reader's own language, and the risk of misunderstanding will be lessened.

In choosing school as a sample community for more detailed analysis I was influenced by the fact that it is the community-form of which I have had most experience, having worked in it for a quarter of a century. It may be objected that it is a mistaken choice, since what is true of children may not be true of adults, or vice versa. The answer is that both are human beings, and that the characteristics of human coexistence are the same in essence, whether the beings be old or young. There is another answer, which may be more convincing, viz. that the forms and conditions of co-operation to which children are accustomed at school are those on which they rely when they go out into the world. It seems clear and indisputable that the methods of our statesmen and politicians in handling international problems —whether in Western Europe, in Asia or in Ireland —are but an expanded version of the public school traditions of the community, in which their discipline and punishment appear in the guise of sanctions. Further to secure the present form of community against change, the gospel of duty and service is preached with increasing fervour in the schools of the poorer citizens.

These things are not without purpose. Those who mishandle our destinies under the pretence of statesmanship are primarily concerned with the maintenance of the present form of community: for this they must be provided with an obedient democracy. On the other hand, those to whom the present form of community secures but a small and diminishing advantage, and heaven knows they are many, must needs remodel it to their greater good. The value of a community may be assessed by the advantage it secures to its individual members: weighed in this balance the communities of Western Europe to-day cannot but be found wanting. If we are to build them anew,—for reconstruction on the old model is our shortest cut to ruin,—if in the process we are to avoid the waste and the insensate destruction of revolution by force, we must have clear in our minds beyond any possibility of error the conditions which are essential to human coexistence. Only after they have been clearly stated can we set about securing them. Vague vapourings about 'a land fit for heroes' no longer serve to drug our reason. Bankrupt in credit, with hunger and unemployment staring us in the face, we need something at once more simple and more drastic than a further loan or the frenzied economies of the spendthrift. We need a community where none go hungry and none are slaves. It does not seem much to ask: it should not be beyond the wit of man to compass this, even though it take a generation or a century. It is no longer a question of making the world safe for democracy: we have to make it safe for humanity, or perish, and give way to some other form of life less ignorant and more adventurous.

* * * * *

PREFACE

It is with profound gratitude that I acknowledge the kindness of the Master of Peterhouse (Sir Adolphus Ward) in reading this slight analysis of coexistence. As a young student under him at the University of Manchester, I first began to understand what scholarship might mean when inspired by sympathy and a comprehension of human needs. None of us who learnt from him can ever forget his wide general outlook and vivid appreciation of essential detail : in attending his lectures we stood on a high hill on a clear day. To have written a treatise which he found interesting is a source of personal happiness : to be allowed to print this criticism of its general line of argument is an honour.

". . . You must not expect an opinion worth having from me, as my equipment in the way of psychological physiology is very small. What is more in my line, is the application of principles or axioms founded on a logical enquiry such as yours, and I do not see why the same hand should not undertake both parts of a double task. In other words, I do not see why you should not have elaborated your Chapter XIII and thus made a bigger book of what is a very notable effort. If you remember (which is highly improbable) anything of my history teaching at Manchester, you may remember a commonplace which I was fond of bringing before my students : History is an account of man living (or working) in communities. This definition was constantly in my mind in considering theories of the *state*—a very different thing; and your treatise has brought the difference out more clearly than I can remember to have seen it brought out before. From this point of view nothing could be more opportune—as well as I think sounder—than your general argument; and I do not see why it should not be fully illustrated, and thus receive a wider attention than it may otherwise attract.

"In any case, I can assure you that your argument has taken hold of me forcibly, and that it is by no means only as a humble supporter of the League of Nations that I think you in the right way.

"Yours very sincerely,
"A. W. WARD."

I can only hope that the following pages may prove of interest and of value—however small—to those who read them, and may help towards a clearer comprehension of the principles of coexistence and co-operation which underlie all human evolution.

R. E. ROPER.

LONDON,
March, 1922.

CONTENTS

	PAGE
PREFACE	5

PART I

THE PHYSICAL NATURE OF MAN

CHAPTER I
MAN A RECEIVER OF STIMULI 19

CHAPTER II
MAN A GENERATOR OF STIMULI 30

CHAPTER III
THE HARMONISING OF VIBRATIONS 42

PART II

DEFINITIONS

CHAPTER IV
THE IMPORTANCE OF CLEAR DEFINITIONS 57

CHAPTER V
DEFINITIONS 64

CHAPTER VI
NOTES ON THE DEFINITIONS 67

CONTENTS

PART III

THE COMMUNITY
(i) EVOLUTION

CHAPTER VII
THE EVOLUTION OF THE COMMUNITY 85

CHAPTER VIII
ANIMAL AND HUMAN COMMUNITIES 94

CHAPTER IX
THE GENERAL PRINCIPLES OF COEXISTENCE . . . 103

PART IV

THE COMMUNITY
(ii) ORGANISATION

CHAPTER X
THE NATURAL CONTROLS OF COEXISTENCE 115

CHAPTER XI
AN INDIVIDUAL AND HIS COMMUNITIES 123

CHAPTER XII
THE COMMUNITY OF SCHOOL 131

PART V

THE COMMUNITY
(iii) DISEASE

CHAPTER XIII
COMMUNITIES AND STATES 147

CONTENTS

CHAPTER XIV
THE DISEASED COMMUNITY 160

CHAPTER XV
THE DISEASES OF AUTHORITY 170

PART VI

THE FUTURE OF MAN

CHAPTER XVI
THE TENDENCY OF THE INDIVIDUAL 185

CHAPTER XVII
THE TENDENCY OF THE COMMUNITY 202

CHAPTER XVIII
PLUS OR MINUS ? 216

BIBLIOGRAPHY 221

INDEX 223

PART I

THE PHYSICAL NATURE OF MAN

CHAPTER I

MAN A RECEIVER OF STIMULI

" Brownian movement "	19
Vibration and movement characteristic of man	21
The growth of the earth	23
The origin of life	24
The habitat of man	25
The limits of vibration	26
Man as a receiver of stimuli	27

CHAPTER II

MAN A GENERATOR OF STIMULI

The movement of protoplasm	30
Movement and life	34
Movement and thought	36
Personality and change	38
Man as a generator of stimuli	40

CHAPTER III

THE HARMONISING OF VIBRATIONS

Harmonising vibrations	42
The latent period	50
Summary of the physical nature of man	54

CHAPTER I

MAN A RECEIVER OF STIMULI

"Brownian Movement."

"When we consider a fluid mass in equilibrium, for example some water in a glass, all the parts of the mass appear completely motionless to us. If we put into it an object of greater density it falls and, if it is spherical, it falls exactly vertically. The fall, it is true, is the slower the smaller the object; but, so long as it is visible, it falls and always ends by reaching the bottom of the vessel. When at the bottom, as is well known, it does not tend again to rise. . . . These familiar ideas, however, only hold good for the scale of size to which our organism is accustomed, and the simple use of the microscope suffices to impress on us new ones. . . . Indeed it would be difficult to examine for long preparations in a liquid medium without observing that all the particles situated in the liquid instead of assuming a regular movement of fall or ascent, according to their density, are, on the contrary, animated with a perfectly irregular movement. They go and come, stop, start again, mount, descend, remount again, without in the least tending toward immobility. This is the *Brownian movement,* so named in memory of the naturalist Brown, who described it in 1827." (Ch. I. § 1.) "What we observe, so long as we can distinguish anything, is not a cessation of the movements, but that they become more and more chaotic. . . . In brief, the examination of Brownian movement alone suffices to suggest that every fluid is formed of elastic molecules animated by a perpetual motion." (Ch. I. § 6.)[1]

In attempting to state as simply as possible the essential characteristics of a human being, this explanation of Brownian movement is of extraordinary value. From the concept of man as a form of life inhabiting this earth we may proceed to assume that his material body is composed of the stuff of which the earth is made. This assumption is common alike to the latest scientific and the earliest religious beliefs, and were man less accustomed to keep his knowledge in watertight compartments the phrase "dust thou art and unto dust shalt thou return" would bring him less of terror and more of dignity and peace as the handful of earth drops into the open grave. The feeling of impermanence and insecurity should be less a cause—as it too often is—of fear and a cowering servitude than an inspiration of joyous adventure as he begins another chapter in the thrilling book of evolution.

We may safely assume that matter groups itself into three main phases, solid, liquid and gaseous, and that these phases are under certain conditions interchangeable; e.g. water may be boiled and

[1] *Brownian Movement and Molecular Reality*, Perrin, translated by Soddy.

give off steam or be frozen and become ice, air under pressure may become liquid and be poured from one receptacle to another, iron may be made liquid when sufficiently heated and may be poured out into moulds where it cools and reassumes its solid phase. And whether gaseous, liquid or solid, the material is characterised by movement, as in the case of fluids Brownian movement, in gases a constant collision and rebound of molecules; in solids the most obvious example is radium, where the streaming off of particles gives the impression of a more than personal activity of inexhaustible power.

VIBRATION AND MOVEMENT CHARACTERISTIC OF MAN.

Since the body of man is composed of the material of the world, and since this material in each of its phases is characterised by movement, unless the phases are so combined in man as to neutralise their movement (which we shall see is not the case [1]) we may conclude that movement and vibration are fundamental human characteristics throughout the whole of life; they are indeed 'being alive.' This assumption is so important that it is worth while to reason it out from another point of view, so as to make more certain that it is correct. The material of this earth, though now more or less definitely grouped in the three phases (solid, liquid and gaseous) must at some period of its history have been otherwise arranged. There are various

[1] " Movement of Protoplasm," p. 30.

theories as to the origin of the earth, some of them, e.g. that in the first chapter of Genesis, more poetically than scientifically stated, yet with a very considerable amount of agreement. Those who wish to study the more scientific theories will find a useful summary of them in the *Geology* of Chamberlin and Salisbury.[1] The two writers then proceed to state what they call the 'planetesimal hypothesis' of the formation of the world. This extremely probable and carefully reasoned argument assumes that our earth and the solar system to which it belongs were torn from some larger mass by the pull of a passing body, and whirled away into space in the shape of a 'spiral nebula.' This is a frequent formation in the sky, and may roughly be described as resembling (in section) a catherine wheel with a cloudy centre (in which the three phases of matter are as yet indistinguishable). From the centre project two portions, one on each side: these, owing to their nature and position, tend to be left a little behind the whirling central mass: they thus wrap themselves round it in a spiral formation.[2] Later on, the material composing the whole—which at first was in a finely-divided and widely-dispersed condition—began to collect into more definite groups or formations, and to settle down into the fixed shapes which as sun, moon, earth, etc., we include in the one phrase 'solar system.'

[1] *Geology*, Chamberlin and Salisbury, vol. ii.
[2] Nebula = a cloud or mist,—as for instance the fine shower of particles given off by a throat-spray.

The Growth of the Earth.

When once the relative positions of the main bodies in this system were determined, the earth began to grow slowly,—partly from the original and still dispersed material and partly by intercepting and attracting other bodies. Its internal temperature rose, and spread outward. Obviously, at this stage of earth-growth our present human life-form cannot have existed: it depends upon constant breathing in and out of certain gases for its continued life, and all the complicated lung-apparatus which we now possess would have been ineffective at this stage, when air as we know it did not exist. Our lungs are a product of later evolution.

The earth-growth passed through various stages. After the settling down of a nucleus there would be a possible period with no atmosphere: this would only be found when the earth developed far enough to be able to attract to itself and to keep its hold on the lighter gases. Then would come a volcanic condition, in which the fiercely-burning core shot out heat and additional gases to mix with those of the previous stage. The central core of stone (lithosphere) would now be surrounded by a gaseous covering (atmosphere): later on there was formed between them a layer of liquid (the hydrosphere). The three phases of material would now be clearly marked, solid within liquid and both inside the gaseous covering. It is remarkable that this process of formation of an inner and an outer covering, with subsequent development of a third or middle layer between them, is repeated in the earlier stages of the development of every human being.

The Origin of Life.

At this stage the 'planetesimal theory' supposes life to have first taken form. There then followed a second stage of volcanic action, or a climax of the first. After this came the period which includes most of our known geologic time, in which atmosphere and hydrosphere influenced and gradually altered the shape of the lithosphere, air and water 'weathering' and softening the sharper contours of the more solid 'earth.'

Whatever stages or periods we postulate, we may take the gradual grouping of the contents of the parent nebula which became earth to have been marked by a constant interchange of phase of material, solid rock being melted in the inner core and poured forth in liquid or gaseous form, gaseous condensing into liquid elements, the whole gradually settling down into three phases, solid, liquid and gaseous, or roughly earth, water and air. Each phase was and is characterised by vibration and movement, slower in the heavier and more dense, swifter in the lighter and more dispersed phase.

How and when the forces which cause life as we know it first took form is a matter for conjecture. It is no solution to suppose that the form already existed in the body from which the parent nebula was torn: this merely pushes the problem a stage further back. Some may prefer to suppose that when the earth was ready for it all the known animals were created in order, ready-made as it were, by God. Others will see no irreverence or irreligion in assuming that as the three concentric spheres arrived at such a stage of growth as to render it possible for a simple life-form to exist, the forces which cause life took on such material shape as was then possible. This is a no less fascinating and no less inspiring theory, and is as much in accord with belief in the omnipotence of God as with the inevitability of natural law. As stated by Chamberlin in a later book [1] there is a feeling of reverence for preordained purpose and a clarity of thought which should appeal to both the 'religious' and the 'scientific' mind. The magnificent simplicity of his reasoning is a piece of mental architecture which should stand for ever as a vindication of the theory of evolution.

THE HABITAT OF MAN.

The three concentric spheres of earth, air and water are not all complete or perfect in shape: they have however surfaces of contact. (For example, a sectional drawing of the Channel between Dover and Calais would show the chalk cliff meeting the water, descending under it and rising again in France. The grass at the top of the down, the face of the cliff, the surface of the waves, the sand and the grass at Calais, are all in contact with the air.) Where the three phases of matter, earth, air and water, touch one another is called a contact-

[1] *The Origin of the Earth*, Chamberlin.

horizon: it is about these contact horizons that life began. They are as it were a zero-line above and below which life soon ceases to be possible. For man especially the distance on each side of the line is very small. Without special contrivances he cannot exist for five minutes below the earth-air or water-air line. Without special contrivances he cannot lift himself his own height above the earth. He cannot without special contrivances raise himself above the earth-water line at all: in this he is beaten by the penguin, who can swim fast enough to shoot himself into the air and land on a block of ice or on a rock several feet above the surface of the sea. Even with the aid of aeroplanes or diving-bells or caissons the limit of compression or decompression to which man may safely be subjected is soon reached. Compared with the diameter of the ball on which he lives his margin of vertical movement is infinitesimally small. In the direction of the North and South Poles however it is possible for him to travel and live in an area almost as large as the whole contact horizon of earth and water with air. His habitat may thus be conceived of as almost world-wide in area but diminutive in depth.

The Limits of Vibration.

In a fascinating chapter of *The Origin of the Earth*,[1] the author pursues the movement of molecules to its utmost limit. "The molecule is a very active little body, always apparently in a whirl or a quiver. . . . Two could scarcely be

[1] *The Origin of the Earth*, Chamberlin.

brought together, however gently, in such a way that they would rest quietly side by side. The whirl or quiver of one or of the other, or both, would be almost sure to send them apart with a sharp recoil. . . . In our atmosphere, the gravity of the earth is always pulling the molecules together." There comes a limit however to the pull of gravity: very far away the pull is less, and in an ultra-atmosphere there will be a stage where the lighter molecules have more room to move. Nearer the centre their paths between collisions are shorter and straighter: further away these become curved and longer, so that they rise and fall like drops of water in a fountain. "The picture is not without its beauty, the whole summit of the atmosphere a mass of vaulting molecules, describing loops of multitudinous forms and dimensions set in all possible directions." Yet even this is not the end: some will escape far enough from gravity to set out on orbits of their own. These again collide amongst themselves and some will be pushed further away: of these some return after a long time, or follow new orbits, or fall into the sphere of attraction of the sun or of other whirling bodies. And finally "the fountain and the orbital phases of the solar atmosphere envelope the atmospheres of all the planets." So movement is not merely common to the three phases of the material of this earth, but is inter-planetary and all-pervading.

Man as a Receiver of Stimuli.

We have seen that, from the centre of the earth to the uttermost limit of the solar system and beyond, each particle of matter is in constant movement and vibration. Interposed between the earth centre and the ultra-atmosphere is the extremely shallow limit in which it is possible for man to exist. Also, the material of which man is composed is fundamentally the same as that of the world on which he lives. Are we to suppose then that by some strange system of insulation he and other life-forms are not ʻsubject to the general principle of vibration which governs earth and air and water? That the heat of the sun should penetrate the air and warm both sea and land, and leave us cold? That there are no rays of light which travel through our tissues and come out the other side? That electricity affects all other known bodies, but passes us by? Are we alone insensible to vibrations? The supposition is absurd. Bodily we are—and what else could we be?—a tiny weight of metal, a little earth and air and water, and we react to any vibration to which these react. Our senses are but special organs developed for the express purpose of receiving vibrations of one kind or another. Within the limits of the compass of our senses we depend absolutely upon our correct perception of rates of vibration for our knowledge of the external world. There are rays of light to which our retina does not react, but such as they are we depend upon our organs of sight for our appreciation of colour, of light and shade, and for much of our space-perception. There are waves of sound too slow or too fast to be registered by our ears, but within their limitations we depend upon them for the reception of speech and music. Our tissues may be destroyed equally by extreme heat or cold, but we depend upon the sense organs located in them for our knowledge of variation of temperature. So with our sense of touch : widespread throughout the body, as well as more definitely localised in tongue and finger-tips, we depend upon it for our appreciation of weight and pressure, and for much of our knowledge of our own position and that of other objects in space. So far from being insensible to vibrations, man is an organism especially developed for the purpose of receiving them.

CHAPTER II

MAN A GENERATOR OF STIMULI

The Movement of Protoplasm.

WHATEVER may have been the stage of earth-growth at which the forces which make life first took form, it seems not unreasonable to suppose that the material upon which they acted ultimately responded by grouping itself into what (for want of a better acquaintance with its properties) has been called protoplasm, or first-material. The most elementary form of life at present known is a single cell: it is definitely separable from its surroundings and has an appreciable internal content. Whether it has an envelope sufficiently clearly marked to be called a skin is not clear: it would perhaps be more accurate to compare its outside surface to that of water standing up beyond the top of an overfilled glass: whatever its nature may be, it is known as its external membrane. It has then what the ordinary man would call an inside and an outside, and it is customary to regard it as the most simple life-form. Examples of it may be found in the apparently green growth which appears on the sunlit surface of standing water (on the contact-horizon of water and air). The desire to see it more closely suggests the use of a

MAN A GENERATOR OF STIMULI

microscope. Now the difficulties inherent in the use of a microscope upon living cells are many and serious: they are well stated by a practised observer (Bayliss [1]) of unrivalled experience. "It is unfortunate that the study of the phenomena presented by living cells is rendered difficult by the fact that so little can be seen by microscopic examination." (Here one has to remember that the sense organ upon which one is depending for receiving an external stimulus is the eye, and that the vibrations received are those of light, reflected from the surface of the object being examined: the appearance of a mother-of-pearl handle of a knife is a good example.) "The presence of different structures in a cell, even supposing that they are colourless, can be detected if they have refractive indices differing from that of the surrounding substance. . . . Now most of the various structures in living cells possess very nearly the same refractive index, a fact which renders this mode of microscopic vision of limited use." It is however possible to stain the substance under examination with certain dyes: this is a regular and standardised technique, under which definite substances react in definite ways, and are even named from their method of reaction. Some of the dyes are unavoidably poisonous and injure or destroy the life of the cell: others produce in the cell structures due to the dye (compare the production of pearl in oysters by introducing foreign matter). "After fixation, neither the form nor the staining properties give correct information

[1] *General Physiology*, Bayliss, ch. I.

32 THE PHYSICAL NATURE OF MAN

as to the relationship of the constituents of the original system." That is as much as to say that without staining the structures are to some extent invisible, and that with staining there is no guarantee that the normal life of the cell can be observed.

Another fundamental source of error in microscopic work arises from the fact that the object observed, however thin, has a certain thickness; also, the lenses have to be moved in order to be focussed. That is to say, the focus may be upon the top or middle or bottom of the object examined. The same author [1] has a series of photographs illustrating this difficulty. A thin metal plate of known thickness has made in it a number of holes regularly arranged: the lenses of the microscope are then moved to the extent of the plate's thickness, the focus thus falling upon various depths of the plate. Photographs of the object as seen at different stages of the process were taken, and form the illustrations in question. Compared with the pattern and appearance of the holes in the original metal plate, they give the impression of something entirely different in structure: one of them, instead of suggesting holes in an object, resembles closely the surface of that patterned glass which is manufactured so that one may not see through a window: another looks like cloth painted with a small black and white check.

As a means of enquiry and research into the origin or properties of protoplasm, one may be excused for regarding microscopic examination as

[1] *General Physiology*, Bayliss, p. 8 f.

at least unreliable. There is a further consideration to be taken into account, viz. that the simplest cell is after all merely the form in which matter reacts to the forces which caused the earliest life to take shape: the attempt to deduce the nature of the force from the appearance of the form is as liable to failure as would be the attempt to deduce the nature of lightning from the appearance of a tree which it has struck. It is possible that some such error of thought is responsible for the very literal and unimaginative materialism which characterises not only many so-called scientists but also (through their influence) the large majority of ordinary men and women. The effect of this upon the mental and spiritual evolution of man is little short of disastrous.

Yet though the origin and nature of protoplasm may not at present be revealed by the microscope, its habits and movements can be easily detected. An amœba may be seen to move, to change its form in response to changes in its surroundings: it can 'go' from place to place, can 'grow' towards its food, surround it and apparently having absorbed nourishment 'grow' past it and leave it behind. Whether this is to be regarded as purposed movement need not be discussed here: one may make a note of it as possibly connected with the movements which in more complex life-forms are known as reflex or unconscious or automatic or instinctive. At any rate this simple cell, which reproduces itself by division, is permeated by that vibration which is common to its ancestral elements. "There is one fact about which there can be no doubt, that is, that protoplasm behaves as a liquid. . . . Further, when the fine particles, present in certain parts of protoplasmic organisms, are examined under the microscope, they are seen to be in constant movement. . . . On the death of the protoplasm the movements cease, and a precipitation or coagulation, like the 'setting' of gelatine when it cools, occurs."[1] We have seen that being in movement is being alive : we may say now that cessation of movement is death.

Movement and Life.

The movement typical of the simple cell is a property of the more complicated cell-groups in which the life-forms of to-day are arranged. Simple amœbic movement occurs in our bodies in the wandering of leucocytes and phagocytes from tissue to tissue : it is found, not as a wandering but as a more stationary advance and retreat, in the gemmules or little buds which spring from the branches of the nerve-trees in our brains, protruding during sleep and retracting during activity.[2] Definite and apparently purposive movement is typical of sperm and ovum in fertilisation. We are characterised by movement from our simplest to our most complex processes. It is this which we have in common with the still water in a glass, with the gold and lead which when left touching one another long enough begin to interchange their particles, with the molecules which stream

[1] *General Physiology*, Bayliss, ch. i.
[2] *Mind and its Disorders*, Stoddart, ch. i.

from one plate to another in an electric battery, with the stars and the many solar systems.

When we examine the individual human being we find movement essential to his development: his whole organism is directly evolved to this end. He moves before and during birth: his movement ceases only when he dies. Without it he cannot breathe, he can neither swallow nor assimilate his food, he cannot maintain the circulation of his blood. Without the movement of thousands of tiny fibrils in his ear he cannot register sound; without movement he cannot speak, he cannot gain a knowledge of space, he cannot direct his eyes toward an object or focus them upon it. Even in sleep his movements must continue, or he dies. Movement is a condition fundamentally necessary to human life, painfully evolved through the countless experiences of age-long evolution from the earliest vibrations of the first living cell, and from those still earlier which pervaded its three ancestral elements. By movement he must gain experience of the external world: should he desire to express himself in any way it is by movement that he must do so. Failing it he lies imprisoned in inactivity, a helpless dying thing: even inactivity is a partial death. In his earliest experiments he gropes and feels his way, a crawling quadruped until experience enables him to stand erect, to walk, to avoid fixed and moving objects, to turn, to run. Constant movement-experience reacts upon his brain, grouping its cells and developing association-paths, rendering habit possible as a labour-saving device, giving him surer control of his own apparatus, bringing him into contact with other human beings and rendering coexistence with them possible. The movements of the violinist and of the bricklayer's labourer differ only in degree and in direction of specialisation : their common factor is the vibration of the living cells of which both are made, their common condition of activity (differing again only in degree) being constant adaptation and recombination of movement. Movement is a condition fundamental to human life, movement and its resulting change.

Movement and Thought.

Consider again the structure of the human brain in its present stage of evolution, an interwoven mass of individual cell-groups, close together yet never actually touching, or so seldom that 'never' is more accurate than 'rarely.' Their general arrangement resembles that of roots and branches in a forest of trees, passing up and down through various layers of substance.[1] Whenever nerve-force, or the vitality of the nerve-cells in a group, is strong enough to pass the intervening space, a nerve-message may be sent leaping from branch to branch. The message-paths most used are the physical basis of habit. It is not as though an actual concrete message were sent, like a squirrel jumping from tree to tree: the movement is a far finer vibration, perhaps among the particles in the protoplasm of one group, communicated in some at present unknown manner to those of

[1] For excellent illustrations see *Nervous Diseases*, Starr.

another. These movements or vibrations permeate the cells of the brain and nervous system, widespread as those among the molecules in water or in the ultra-atmosphere, occurring not in one place or direction only but in many, with countless possibilities of permutation and combination. Such is the ' machine ' by which we deal with one another, a variously vibrating community of cells, each quivering in response to the vibrations through space, to those received from other life-forms, to those which it in itself generates, each exhausting its own powers with the effort of its own existence and constantly being rebuilt. Vibration and movement are characteristic of the central nervous system as they are of other human organs : they would even seem to be characteristic of the modes of human thought.

Take, for example, the ' bell-concept ' of Charcot, in which he summarises the various stimuli, sensations and memories which go to make up the human concept of ' bell.' The weight, touch, temperature, appearance, sound of the actual bell, the shape and sound of the word ' bell,' the sensations of writing and speaking and hearing the word, the drawing of the object, the memories, stimuli and associations connected with these, and so on. Admit that any one of these may call up or suggest any one or any group of the others, and you have a condition directly comparable to the vibrations of Brownian movement. Suppose each one of the above to be a molecule or particle, and each free to vibrate, then when one collides against another they may combine to form a thought or partial concept of bell: not all need be included in this or at the same time, but one will 'rise into consciousness' and fall again; one may collide with other memories or associations and there rises up another concept or train of thought: this in turn may arouse a third, and so *ad infinitum* but for paths and habits of associations previously formed, or the power of attention and concentration at the disposal of the thinker.

Personality and Change.

Even human personality, in its bodily expression at least, is subject to movement and change. John Doe and Richard Roe are no fixed and tangible substances such as yellow orange, or a red pillar-box: numerous troubles and tragedies would be avoided if this were more generally appreciated. It would be bad enough to go out to post the letters and find that the pillar-box had 'come alive' and was opening and shutting its blue-grey mouth in a hungry fashion: it is much worse to come in from a matinée and find that a different person seems to be living inside your husband or your son. These are extreme examples, yet in varying degree this sort of thing takes place from day to day. Not merely are the cells of which John and Richard are composed in constant activity, their brain-content ever changing, their thought processes in almost permanent vibration, but—in the light of recent psychological research—their very personalities are seen to fluctuate and alter. So John may perhaps lose his memory of John, and achieve a fresh combination of his component tendencies, becoming for all practical purposes another being. Or Richard may—with complete sincerity—disappear from his accustomed place and be discovered at another, living in all innocence another life. It is as though both were but the average of their mentality and that this average should change with the fluctuation of their mental processes. As with the composite photographs of public men, in which the superimposed features give a general resemblance with no definiteness of outline, the personality of man is rarely so clearcut as to be always recognisable. Indeed, it is almost more by the regularity of their changes than by their permanent characteristics that we know our friends.

The process of change may be as follows. The mind being full of various concepts or groups of thoughts, attention or desire or an external stimulus may cause them to be grouped in a regular design; the more regular the design, or sequence of association, the more well marked the habit of behaviour. A common example is the man who by the daily repetition of the stimuli of alarm-clock, razor, bath, breakfast and boots is conducted in safety every morning to the station and the office: he is bound by a delicate and strong—though breakable—chain. There may come a time, indeed there often does come a period which is neither sleeping nor waking but a half-way house, in which attention is dispersed and memory hardly roused, when no one group of mind-contents is in definite prominence. In an extreme case of such a state an apparently chance stimulus, or an unexpected shock, may cause an unusual regrouping of thought and memory, with the result that the office is not reached.

Just so may a group of molecules in the ultra-atmosphere have established their positions relative to the earth, when they are disturbed by the impact of another: they may settle down again as before, or regrouping themselves pass beyond the influence of the earth's gravity and drift towards the moon.

Man as a Generator of Stimuli.

Not only do cells respond to stimulus from without: in certain cases they may generate a stimulus from within, which passes over to other cells and may result in movement. A marked example is the electric fish, which has specialised in the action of a particular group of cells to such an extent that it is capable of discharging a shock of sufficient strength to discommode (or even seriously to damage) the disturbing object. In man, the result of the internally generated stimulus or vibration may be confined to his own body, as when one swallows a mouthful of tea: it may even not result in definite movement, but be inhibited, as when one thinks that a cup of tea would be nice, yet goes on working: it may be transferred directly to another body, as when one picks up a cup of tea from a table,—or indirectly through a medium such as air, as when one asks " Can I have some more ? " Examples may be compiled indefinitely: for instance, the vibrations of air caused by the movement of the vocal chords and stimulated by the speech centres in the brain may be transmitted through a resonant disc to the particles of matter in a coherer, from thence to an intermittently excited electrical contrivance, along or round a wire of almost any length until by reversal of these processes they excite the drum of the ear of the friend to whom one is telephoning. A later organisation of vibrations has eliminated the wire, but the process remains the same, i.e. communication by vibrations originally generated within the individual and transferred to the external world. They may be exaggerated in their effect through a megaphone, or translated into an accepted convention of lines and curves called writing, sent to the other side of the world and laid in the light, where their interference with its vibration produces the desired effect upon the eye of the reader, and so upon his brain. The mechanical intermediate movements and vibrations are merely extensions of activities which originally were physical. Their object is to economise physical effort and to multiply its effect: it is a perverted civilisation which allows them to enslave the human beings whose advantage they should serve.

Whatever the activity upon which man is engaged, he depends for communication with the outer world upon the vibrations and movement, the interchange of impulse, which pervades the elements from which he was evolved. Throughout every moment of his existence he is not only a receiver but a generator of vibrations.

CHAPTER III

THE HARMONISING OF VIBRATIONS

Harmonising Vibrations.

In regulating a 'grandfather's' clock, the weight on the end of the pendulum is moved up or down; the shorter the distance between it and the centre upon which it swings, the quicker the swing; to slow the clock the weight is moved further down the rod. To set two clocks so that they may keep exactly together, the weights must be accurately arranged. The difficulty of this process with even a few clocks is enormous. In the case of an engine where the load is constantly changing, the 'governor' acts as an automatic harmoniser of engine-revolutions and load. With a new engine, where some of the parts may be rather a tight fit, the driver expects to spend some time running it in, so that the discordant vibrations due to friction may be overcome and the engine run sweetly. Probably he will find a critical speed, at which the engine runs best: it is the speed at which the vibrations of the moving parts are best harmonised. Some motor-buses and taxis at present plying for hire take years off the life of the driver by the discords they produce: an effective Ministry of Health would insist on their being overhauled

THE HARMONISING OF VIBRATIONS 43

or withdrawn from service, and a general public with a desire for harmony would leave them empty.[1]

Those who have used a public call office for telephoning will appreciate the difficulty of harmonising their own vibrations so as to obtain the best result from their machine. The constant stimuli from extraneous sounds, the buzzing of the wires, the interruptions to the call, the necessity of politeness to the operator at the exchange, the sense of stifling produced by the size of the box, the note upon which they pitch their own voice, these and many other stimuli call for a concentrated attention, a power of inhibition, an incessant variation of effort (to say nothing of the extension of their personality now to the exchange, now to the individual who replies " Wrong number," and at last to the friend or other person at the end of the wire), which should convince them once for all not only that man is a receiver and a generator of vibrations, but that—if he is to produce an effective result—he must harmonise the vibrations of which he is the victim.

The above is so much the knowledge of everyday life that human beings tend to take it for granted : they are however less easily convinced when required to apply the theory to the internal vibrations of others, especially should these be children, employés or enemies. Man, being as it were a focus of vibration, cannot exist in a state of discord, and cannot long endure without disturbance what is discordant.

[1] Compare "The ship that found herself," Kipling (*The Day's Work*).

The difficulty arises over the decision as to discord or concord : who is to say to what note the instrument is to be keyed ? Obviously only the individual can say what is in harmony with himself or to what he may be tuned : this however implies that control is from within, a doctrine not readily accepted at present, and one which has far-reaching consequences.

That the process of harmonising internal vibrations is one that takes time will be more readily admitted. It is the main occupation of childhood and adolescence, and it provides continuous occupation for most adults. It would not be too much to say that only those who are in tune with the infinite, or have a profound religious conviction, or are in harmony with those vibrations which originally caused life to inform the matter of the earliest cell, or in the simpler though more old-fashioned phrase are 'at peace with God,' can consistently achieve harmony. Most of us will to the end of our days be fully occupied with the resolution of our more insistent discords.

It is of the very first importance in the practical organisation of communities, and in reducing friction in daily coexistence with others, to have stated clearly for oneself the theory of the harmonising of vibrations in an individual. The fertilised cell vibrates with the vital energy of both parents : there are other vibrations to which it responds which we may consider later. As it grows and develops it must achieve harmony if it is to attain healthy birth. (It is an error to think of an embryo as a part of its mother : it is an organism engaged upon its own evolution.) Both before and after birth it is sensitive to discord, which it must resolve or become itself discordant. Through its earliest years especially it must be helped toward harmonious growth and strengthened in its powers of resolution in every possible way. Until at least the term of full physical growth, about the age of twenty-four, it should cause no surprise that an individual should find it hard or temporarily impossible to maintain his harmony or even to achieve it at all. One looks with horror at the strain imposed upon the individual by home conditions (none the more suitable because money is plentiful), by school-life, the load of responsibility shouldered at examination time, the constant overstimulation and fatigue, the lack of privacy and the lack of sleep. The most sincere and the most conscientious are those who succumb most easily: there is a special strain imposed on those who fill positions of responsibility (prefects, monitors and the like). When, before internal harmony has been satisfactorily achieved, the immature are drafted into the Army and undergo the destructive strains of war, the gods themselves must stop their ears to shut out the jangled riot of pain which rises from our inferno as it whirls on its path through space. It seems incredible that external authority, in the guise of loving parents or kindly teachers or a paternal government, should be so evil: perhaps it is mere stupidity and ignorance. If so, there is an ignorance more criminal and more devilish in its consequences than even deliberate cruelty.

The development of self-control and the

harmonising of vibrations are one and the same process: it is closely bound up with and—very frequently—has the same crises as the progress of physical growth. The period between conception and birth is of enormous (and usually disregarded) importance. The first year of life, with its incessant beating of external stimuli upon the delicate, sensitive nervous system, is one in which the individual is hard put to it to maintain an internal harmony. Little help is given it by those sentimental and foolish relatives and friends who kiss and fondle it and shake rattles and make stupid conversations in an unintelligible tongue: they never understand that an infant in a cradle may be working as hard as possible at establishing a proper relation between the stimuli from without which demand constant attention and those which arise within its body and call imperatively for control. There is the difficulty of learning language; an enormous amount has to be done in comprehending sound and associating it with meaning before ever pronunciation can be mastered. The control of digestion and of the muscles used in walking are comparatively simple matters compared with speech and the mental processes which precede it.

Particularly under conditions of modern civilisation the period of childhood is one of constant strain, a fact consistently disregarded by parents and teachers. The actual business of living is an occupation for which too little allowance is made, and it is extremely rare for the child's own diagnosis of its condition to be accepted. Yet no

THE HARMONISING OF VIBRATIONS

safer guide to the establishment of internal harmony could be conceived. The tendency to rely on external authority and punishment increases as the individual grows older, in direct opposition to the principles governing creation. It is as though God, having made the world, should push it with his finger to make it travel faster, or alter its axis by a sudden jerk. No wonder the average child arrives at the next crisis of growth in a state of nervous discord, represented on graphs of development by a drop followed by a rise in height or weight. There appears to be no real parallel to this in the animal world. Overstrain at the age of puberty in either sex would be avoided if the preconceived standards of adults were subordinated to the child's own efforts to maintain that internal harmony which—consciously or unconsciously—is its real aim.

The last period of physical development (they may be divided roughly and somewhat inaccurately into three periods of seven years each) is spent in meeting further external strain before the organism is fitted for it. Either the children of poorer parents set out to earn their living, or those of richer ones are prepared for examinations. There is a period between sixteen and nineteen in which the graph of height and weight of many individuals shows a line which resembles that of a particle influenced by Brownian movement: it seems incredible that a superficial observation should still content those who are responsible for children of this age. Standing at a point where their physical evolution draws to a close and their mental capabilities are unfolding, their internal harmony is constantly disturbed, and now more than ever they are in need of help.

The period of growth should be aimed first and foremost at the development of internal harmony, and to this development the one sure guide is the individual himself. He alone can tell what is in harmony with himself and what discordant: he alone can be the ultimate judge of what he may or may not do. This follows naturally from the history of his creation and his existence: it is a fundamental condition of his being. It is common knowledge that a note of music may cause a glass to echo, to shudder, or if sufficiently in discord with its internal harmony may shatter it to pieces. This is a good example of the possible result of punishment. It is a commonplace of mental science that discord in personality or emotion may injure or even destroy mind or body. The permanence of a discordant combination of vibrations (a thought-complex) may cause disastrous results to mental balance, which can only be avoided by a successful resolution of the discord and its recombination into a harmony. An example of the failure of external authority to produce such resolution will always remain in the minds of those who study Dr. Charles Goring's inquiries into criminality.[1] It is the case of a prisoner convicted—as he thought—unjustly: in protest he ceased almost entirely to act as a generator of vibrations. In other words " he refused to work, or to take any food. He was artificially fed for eighteen months:

[1] *The English Convict*, Goring, note 3, p. 251.

THE HARMONISING OF VIBRATIONS 49

and the only real ground for his final certification was his extraordinary manifestation of extreme obstinacy of purpose." (Note: certification, i.e. as insane.)

This is an extreme case, but—varying only in degree—the history of youth and of education is blotted with countless incidents of the kind.

The slow progress of evolution has been toward the increased complication of vibrations received and generated by a single individual (e.g. the development of the nervous system): this has been accompanied by the gradual harmonising of their chaotic nature. These two processes have been facilitated by the improvement of the individual and by the combination of individuals into groups. The formation of groups or communities has invariably been the most advantageous method for securing further development of the individual: the effort toward combined action is itself an aid to the harmonising of vibration. Supposing a quantity of particles to be in a state of vibration such as characterises the molecules in a glass of water,[1] the coherence of some of them into a group will have two effects: (1) they will to some extent be freed from the effect of the impact of other non-combined particles, (2) their coherence will be ensured only by the harmony of the vibrations of the components of the group. Both these consequences will react favourably upon the internal harmony of the individual particles. That the group should be permanent is neither necessary nor desirable: groups will continuously be in a

[1] See "Brownian Movement," Ch. I.

state of building up and breaking down. This is the movement or vibration characteristic of group-existence: it is the group-form of that vibration and movement which characterises the individual particles which compose it.

There is a further problem connected intimately with internal harmony of the individual, viz. that of the course of human evolution. Neglecting for the moment the theory that all human evolution is essentially that of the soul, it will be sufficient to say that its present manifestations tend to show themselves more as changes in the nervous system than in the rest of the body. According to some observers [1] the structure of the body would appear to be reverting rather than advancing, whilst the changes in the nervous system tend to an increase of irritability and a quicker response to stimulus: i.e. the nervous system, whilst becoming a more delicately-balanced mechanism, is also becoming more liable to disturbance and to derangement. If this be true, it is but a further proof of the importance of internal harmony to the individual, as a ' governor ' which shall help him to adapt output of energy to the strain of a varying load.

THE LATENT PERIOD.

Coexistence with others may prove an aid to internal harmony. Plainly, some can coexist with many and others only with a few: all have variations at different stages of evolution, and each needs some time alone in which to recuperate.

[1] *Organic Evolution*, Lull.

THE HARMONISING OF VIBRATIONS

Whenever two individuals meet (i.e. begin to coexist), or, being together, receive a new stimulus, there occurs for a short time what may be called a 'latent period.' Normally both individuals at once tend to harmonise their own vibrations to the utmost, in order to receive or generate further vibrations. Most animals show it very clearly: it is wrong to suppose that they tend to attack or to run away at once; what they actually do first is to be still. The existence of this period seems to have escaped many observers: this is unfortunate, as its importance in human and other coexistence is impossible to exaggerate. It may be considered a latent period even if only one of the pair recognises it; it may be stressed, prolonged, or used, or disregarded. Let us take two examples.

(1) As I write, after breakfast, a wasp flies into the room and settles on my right thumb, on which is still a trace of marmalade. Having for some time made a habit of observing the latent period, I remain still. He rubs his hands, vibrates from head to tail, and proceeds to clean my thumb for me, which I should have done for myself. The habit command 'still' has become automatic and arouses no associations in my mind, but the appearance of the yellow cone-shaped tail of the visitor does. A thought-complex grouped round 'sting' vibrates into activity: I feel an instinctive message—inhibited—quiver down my spinal muscles as I lean over the table: I am conscious of a still hand and a busy wasp against a background of white paper. After a moment or so I

hold my hand near the open window and blow the wasp away.

(2) This is the case of a small and irritable child whose internal harmony was intermittent and almost non-existent at times. Each of us aroused discord in the other until coexistence and co-operation became quite impossible, and the result upon other members of the community was extremely disturbing. After trying every means to improve affairs except punishment (which merely weakens the will of one by subordinating it to that of another) there seemed to be nothing left but permanent irritation. As a last resort we discussed the possibility of doing something to prevent our being always about-to-quarrel, and arranged to smile whenever we met, so as to save trouble. Hurrying past the next day without noticing, a voice called out " Hi ! you've forgotten something ! " and we both found ourselves amused with each other. Not till long afterwards did I realise that we were trying to use a latent period to the best advantage.

There is a whole art of life in the proper use of this period. With practice in it one may travel half across the Continent and through three *douanes* with no trouble and with help from everyone. The old-fashioned name for it was ' being polite ' : it is however something deeper than this, and as ancient as life itself. It may be the skilled and conscious—or better still the instinctive and unconscious—technique of the physical instrument on which we play. It is the first foundation of co-operative effort, just as it is the natural basis of all coexistence. To fail to appreciate its value, to fail to recognise the moment when it comes, is often little short of disastrous. To do this three or four times in a day is a sure indication that one is not fit to be out at all, and a warning to be extremely tactful on the way home, and to rest well on arriving there.

The latent period may be used by a group of people as well as by an individual. It might for instance be consciously employed by representatives of various countries in an international conclave: successful use of it would avoid the possibility of war. Unfortunately its misuse is more frequent, and there is one whole group of people who spend every effort in attempting to influence its outcome, to the disadvantage of another group. An excellent example may be found in the insidious and skilful propaganda by which the Press alienates the middle-class mind from the working class and its needs, so that at a given moment the former may provide a defence force or a white army to control the latter.

SUMMARY OF THE PHYSICAL NATURE OF MAN

THE whole solar system is permeated by vibrations. Vibration and movement are characteristic of the material in which man's physical nature is manifested. Every cell in his body is in a state of vibration: his sense-organs are specially evolved for the reception of vibrations of various kinds. Not only does he receive them from without; he also generates them within him. Movement and change are conditions essential to his continued existence, and typical even of his mode of thought.

In order to fit himself to receive and to generate vibrations, man must evolve within himself an internal harmony between his own vibrations. The period of physical growth is one of constant effort toward this end.

In common with other life-forms man exhibits the phenomenon of the latent period, i.e. a period of non-activity marked by a definite effort toward internal harmony. The proper use of this period is essential to successful coexistence, whether of individuals or of groups.

Internal harmony and self-control are identical in their nature. The attempt to substitute external authority for either is in the end disastrous.

PART II

DEFINITIONS

CHAPTER IV

THE IMPORTANCE OF CLEAR DEFINITIONS
    Some results of misunderstanding 59
    'Science' and 'religion' 61

CHAPTER V

DEFINITIONS 64

CHAPTER VI

NOTES ON THE DEFINITIONS 67
    Summary of Part II 81

CHAPTER IV

THE IMPORTANCE OF CLEAR DEFINITIONS

WHEN I send my bicycle to be overhauled and 'done up,' I tie a luggage-label on to the handle-bars with this sort of inscription: "Fit new front brake, shorten chain: fit new blocks to back brake: stove all black: heat front forks." This is clear, and in the popular tongue: the last phrase is a species of Esperanto. My machine is old, I ride it hard, and depend on it daily: the rough roads cause a localised vibration of the front forks under which the molecules in the material tend to assume a new relationship less adapted to resist strain, and I have no desire to be impaled on them when they snap. I think it to be a form of crystallisation and I cannot remember the technical word for the antidote: the cycle-repairer knows all this. So we compromise by a phrase which conveys a sufficiently accurate meaning to both of us. It is a simple matter when one is dealing with a machine: were the bicycle alive it would be very different.

Consider the question of pain. A and B break their lower arm on two consecutive Fridays. A is a week ahead of B in rebuilding his bones, and each week gains at least a day on B's rate of recovery. The fractures are similar enough to be regarded as equally injurious, yet B has more pain than A. The restriction of shoulder movement owing to a habit-position due to wearing a sling is slight in A: in B it amounts to a 50 per cent. rigidity. I wish to explain this, and to suggest reasons for the difference, to a student; among our words and phrases are 'standard of pain,' 'memory,' 'nervous system,' 'general vitality,' 'mind,' 'imagination,' 'fear,' 'shock,' as well as such definite technical terms as abduction, pronation, etc. The latter are comparatively simple, because they deal with mechanism. To obtain a reasonable accuracy with the former, I have to allow for my knowledge of the student and of A and B, as well as for the vagueness of the terms and the impossibility of accurately assessing the pain of one individual, and the equal impossibility of stating A's pain in terms of B's sensibility.

The difficulty is multiplied indefinitely when I wish to discuss C, a 'nervous' and 'unsatisfactory' child,[1] with others who teach him: they may use such words as 'troublesome,' 'undisciplined,' 'lacking in a respect for the community,' 'slovenly'; they will state C in terms of the effect he has upon themselves. At the best, one of us may say that his 'power of attention' is not as great as it might be: at least this is a step towards the definition of C in terms of himself. But what is 'attention'? Its symp-

[1] Cf. "Latent Period," Ch. III.

toms may be easily confused with those of idleness, absent-mindedness, fatigue, obedience or fear: suppose these traps to have been avoided, what is 'attention'? One may say that it is a state of mind which fluctuates in value in direct proportion to the interest and the vitality of the individual. Well then, what is 'interest,' and what is 'vitality'? If we are to discuss the overhauling of C, we must have some accuracy in the statement of his needs, and some agreed meaning to the terms we use at least as definite and intelligible as that of the words in which we ask for a bicycle to be repaired.

Some Results of Misunderstanding.

Lacking a word-coinage of fixed value, we proceed to bargain over the present and future of a fellow human-being with the assurance born of habit. Small wonder if we occasionally fail to diagnose his needs. Still, the harm if any is confined to one individual only, unless we include ourselves. But what is to be said of the lighthearted jargon, the easy clichés, with which we organise the present and mortgage the future of whole communities? Few of those in authority have any acquaintance with a theory of evolution, fewer would consider such an abstraction as having any practical bearing on the present, fewer still have either the time or will to begin an experiment which may not show a result for a generation. Yet what is a generation in the history of these islands? The chalk of the North and South Downs was once an unbroken layer between Lewes and Sevenoaks: before that it was slowly deposited by millions of tiny organisms which died and left the lime of their bodies at the bottom of the sea. It was then thrust up above the level of the waves, and through another million years was smoothed away by sea and frost and wind and soft rain, leaving exposed the present watershed of Hastings Sand, upon which Ashdown Forest grew. At some such speed the coexistence of man has been developed; the forces which caused it to take form were as simple as those of frost and rain and the waves of the sea. Its gradual action exposes to view the lifeless skeletons of past organisms of man's creation, those mental missing links, half man half monkey, which once were the high-water mark of his evolution,—'authority,' 'law and order,' 'discipline,' and above all 'the community.' These are the scattered bones amongst which our statesmen grabble like ants, snatching a thighbone here, a shoulder there, and the vertebræ of several spines, with which to set up the composite skeleton of a League of Nations. Impossible to persuade them that the Thames and the Rhine were once tributaries of a common estuary, and that the North Sea (instead of separating them) has merely brought them closer and shortened the voyage from London to Cologne: impossible to convince them that these physical changes have had their parallel in mental evolution. They are obsessed by the thought-complexes of the past, and repression is their only cure for life. It would be hope-

THE IMPORTANCE OF CLEAR DEFINITIONS

less to try to prove to them that it is in spite of and not because of these that human coexistence still evolves.

If we are to avoid a repetition of those dark ages in which former social upheavals have buried civilisation and obliterated wisdom, we must discover and state as clearly and simply as may be the forces which cause human beings to take the form of communities. They are identical with the forces which once caused the triple-phased material of this world to take the life-form of the earliest simplest cell. The human beings which compose the community stand to it in the relation of protoplasmic material to the amœba as a whole. They respond to all-pervading vibration, and the condition essential to their continued existence is freedom of movement and change. Like protoplasm, when movement ceases they die, 'setting' like gelatine when it cools [1] into that coma of standardised effort which is the prelude of organised decay.[2]

'Science' and 'Religion.'

The evolution of the physical nature of man goes hand in hand with the evolution of his idea of God. There is something wilfully blind about that so-called scientific mentality which in the past refused to consider the influence of religion upon human development. The air we breathe,

[1] Cf. "Movement of Protoplasm," Part I, Ch. II, p. 34.
[2] It would seem that these symptoms are common alike to extreme conservatism and to the Socialist State as at present conceived.

the food we eat, the fuel we consume, these apparently are legitimate subjects of enquiry: but the faith of man apparently is to be dismissed as a childish bogy, too vague for serious thought. Yet, whether man makes his God as he progresses, or—as he progresses—becomes more capable of comprehension, whether the soul be a later evolution of perfected thought or the original cause of evolution, the fact that every race of man at apparently every stage of evolution has 'believed in God' and had some concept, however vague, of man's immortal part, is evidence enough to be weighed by the common sense of men and women [1] against the cold analyses of all the professors in the world. For, in considering human coexistence, belief—however 'superstitious'—will be found to play at least as large a part in policy and the decision of action as economic need. The science of coexistence has as its subject-matter the activities of mankind: and in so far as human beings believe in the existence of the soul the soul becomes to that extent concrete and as important as any gas or crystal. And should the patient and somewhat unimaginative scientist decide that the forces which first informed life have much in common with the vibrations of light and air, the men and women whom they teach may see in light but one more manifestation of God, and in the air which they inspire a symbol of the Spirit. The student of sociology and civics must then include the human belief in God in his enquiry: for,

[1] Preface, p. 8.

THE IMPORTANCE OF CLEAR DEFINITIONS

though gropingly and in a glass darkly, it is in accordance with their idea of God that—even to-day—the great majority of men and women and children strive to order the activities of both the individual and the community.

CHAPTER V

DEFINITIONS [1]

1. Human being. An eternal being which for the purpose of its own evolution occupies a life-form of the human type.
2. Spirit or Soul. Terms used to denote the eternal being as distinct from its temporary life-form.
3. Evolution. The progress of the eternal being.
4. Life. A temporary stage in the evolution of the eternal being.
5. Life-force. That which makes alive; a property of the eternal being which has enabled it to evolve its present life-form, and alone secures its further evolution.
6. Life-form. That body in which the soul is made manifest during life.
7. Death. A state in which the life-form has finally ceased to respond to any stimulus.
8. Stimulus. Any change of vibration which produces a corresponding change in a living cell.
9. Nervous system. That part of the life-form which receives, co-ordinates and generates stimuli.

[1] These definitions give the meanings attached to these words in this book.

DEFINITIONS

10. Brain. The centre of the nervous system.
11. Mind. The action of the nervous system.
12. Memory. A tendency (produced by repeated or exaggerated stimuli) in the cells or groups of cells of the nervous system to vibrate in a certain way.
13. Personality. The combined response of spirit and body to vibration.
14. Will. The control of the eternal being over its temporary life-form.
15. Growth. The product of the self-generated processes of bodily or spiritual activity.
16. Community. The association of two or more human beings for common (though not of necessity identical or similar) purpose or advantage in their evolution.
17. Authority. The claim of one human being to control another.
18. Discipline. The exercise of control by one human being over another.
19. Punishment. The means by which discipline is maintained in the face of opposition.
20. Self-control. The attainment of an internal harmony sufficient to enable the reception or generation of stimuli to be varied by the will.
21. Obedience. The submission of one will to another.
22. Instinct. A mind-habit which in past or present life has proved sufficiently of use to the life-form to be incorporated in it as an integral vibration.
23. Habit. A mind-process repeated sufficiently

often between a group or groups of cells to render a certain response to a given stimulus almost inevitable.
24. Reflex action. A reaction to stimulus so completely incorporated in the life-form as to function without an element of consciousness.
25. Law. An agreement between the members of a community so as to facilitate their common purpose.
26. Tradition. The handing on of methods of combination which have been found to be of use.
27. Education. The provision of conditions suitable to further evolution.
28. Thought. The inter-vibration of nerve-cells in the process of analysing, associating and co-ordinating the stimuli transferred to them.
29. Attention. The securing of internal harmony among the vibrations of certain cells or groups of cells so as to facilitate the reception or generation of stimuli.
30. Latent period. The securing of internal harmony of the whole individual so as to facilitate the reception or generation of stimuli.
31. Health. A condition of harmonious vibration.
32. Disease. A condition of discordant vibration.

CHAPTER VI

NOTES ON THE DEFINITIONS

1. Human being. *Eternal.* If the general belief of the human race in immortality is not considered sufficient ground for this assumption, and if such authorities (in the historical sense of the word) as Christ and Buddha and the compilers of the *Book of the Dead* are rejected, those who deny the eternal in man will still find that all that part of this book which deals with the organisation of human coexistence in communities remains applicable.
2. Spirit or soul. The word 'psyche' and its derivatives, 'psychic' and 'psychology,' etc., are examples of the need of a definite terminology. Liddell and Scott give the following meanings: I (1) breath = life = spirit, (2) things dear as the very life; II (1) the life or spirit of man which survives after death = departed soul = spirit = ghost, (2) the abstract notion of the soul or spirit of man, (3) the seat of the will, desires and passions = the inmost soul = the heart, (4) sensual desire, propension, appetite, used also of animals; III (1) the organ of thought and judgment = soul

= mind = reason = understanding, (2) the spirit of an author; IV (1) the vital principle, (2) the *anima mundi* or animating spirit of the Universe, supposed *ire per omnes terrasque tractusque maris cœlumque profundum* (in the most ancient philosophers); V, a butterfly, because it is an emblem of the immortal soul by reason of its passing through a kind of death in the chrysalis form; VI, Psyche, the mistress of Eros (or Love), represented in art with butterfly's wings or as a butterfly. Some twenty meanings in all.

"Psychology" is, we may suppose, the study of the mind. In defining 'mind' as 'the action of the nervous system' (definition 11) I am aware that this implies that the study of mind includes the study of physiology: my contention is that it does and should so include it. Any textbook of mental diseases does so. I should go further and say that the study of the mind should always include the study of the soul, which is far from being the case. The majority of textbooks of psychology, by divorcing the studies of soul and body from that of mind, present in my opinion an arid desert of abstractions to the student and crowd his brain-content with a mass of artificiality. This is not the least striking example of that materialistic concept of science which has devastated modern life by specialising in the processes of death.

NOTES ON THE DEFINITIONS

Let us try to classify the above meanings of psyche according to the theories of creation and evolution as stated in Part I.

VIBRATIONS

Interplanetary and All-pervading	As manifested in—		
	(A) body	(B) mind	(C) soul
	I (1)	III (1)	I (1)
	II (4)		II (1)
			II (2)
			II (3)
IV (1)			
IV (2)			

V and VI may be included in A and B, or omitted. On this showing, psyche may mean the original vibrations which pervaded space before this solar system was torn from its parent sphere, or it may mean the soul which goes on after life has stopped, or it may mean the mind which is manifested physically through the action of the brain and nervous system: that is, it may mean (1) something temporary or something eternal, (2) something individual or something all-pervading, (3) something human or something divine, (4) something original or something later evolved. Neither (2), (3) nor (4) are mutually exclusive, and only (1) seems to cancel out. For myself, I should prefer to regard the all-pervading vibration as either God or an early manifestation of God,—soul or spirit as the eternal or divine component of the human being,—taking 'elemental' to mean the earlier (and perhaps therefore more material) phase of evolution which we have had in common with other life-forms (e.g. dogs and other animals, etc.). I should regard the 'organ of thought and judgment' as being essentially elemental, physical and material, a group of cells specialised for a definite purpose, including both brain and central and peripheral nerves.

Having been asked " What shape would the soul take after the death of the body ? " I do not know. But if vibrations may be altered by combination with other vibrations or by the interposition of material substances, and if individual effort to establish internal harmony has been successful, it might be credible that on the death and dissolution of the material body the vibrations should persist. The soul would then be expressed in a new vibration-rate, and, meeting material which was in a condition which rendered it responsive to this new series of vibrations, might cause it to cohere

NOTES ON THE DEFINITIONS 71

into a life-form. This may offend those who believe in re-incarnation, as being too materialistic; it will almost certainly offend the scientific mind as being impossible or ridiculous. I can only hope that the child who asked me the question may find the answer for himself.

3. Evolution. The progress (usually toward a greater complexity) not only of the soul but of the body or life-form. It is not necessary to discuss here which causes which.

4. Life. This may have another meaning than a mere period of time, viz. in the phrase "Life was extinct." This I have preferred to include under definition 5.

5. Life-force. Either the all-pervading vibrations, the *anima mundi* of the ancient philosophers, able *ire per omnes terrasque tractusque maris cœlumque profundum* (the three phases of the material of the world),—or that from which the vibrations originally emanated, their cause. Some will prefer to call this God.

6. Life-form. This phrase is preferable to 'human being': it makes room for every animal and other form of life, even crystals (as being material grouped into a definite separable shape in response to some vital power, though not possessing movement as we know it). There is sufficient room in the study of evolution for the theories of St. Francis concerning birds and beasts, and for his hymn to the Creator, as for

the latest handbook on embryology or comparative osteology or anatomy.

It seems incorrect to consider body as limited by skin or external membrane. 'Bodily' includes all excretions (perspiration is a crude example) which contain bodily or elemental material in any of the three phases: it should properly then include emanations of the same kind, such as odours. Another group not wholly bodily, in which the vibrations of the bodily material are transferred to other elements, would include such electrical and other manifestations as may be considered to exist, e.g. telepathic, or of the nature of thought transference, or connected with what is known as the aura of the individual, or with 'ghosts.' Such manifestations I should prefer to include under the general term 'elemental.'

8. Stimulus. *Any change of vibration.*

A. This would seem to imply that a series of vibrations is not perceived unless it is a new one. This, of course, is not the case: the problem may be complicated in many ways. For instance, I am in a room in which a clock ticks every second: if during an experiment I have to close a switch every forty seconds, I shall hear many ticks very clearly, though at the last I shall become inaccurate. If in the same room I sit and read a book, I shall hear the clock intermittently, irregularly, or even not at

NOTES ON THE DEFINITIONS 73

all. Again, if I use a pungent preparation of rubber to fill the cuts in the outer cover of a tyre, it may offend my nose for a minute or even two, but soon I shall not smell it at all. Attention and fatigue both play a part in these results. But the vast majority of stimuli may be classified under the heading 'change of vibration,' so I have preferred to omit the rest.

B. In this connection are to be considered pleasure, pain, shock, and the like. (1) Pleasure, that which is or produces a vibration-rate harmonious to that of the life-form. (2) Pain, that which is itself discordant or produces discord, or is excessive. Either (1) or (2) may produce the fatigue described in A: also, (1) may become (2) through repetition. (3) Shock: an excessive and sudden form of either (1) or (2). Also, (1) or (2) may lead to (2) or (1) by cessation of the vibration which caused it.

9. Nervous system. It is usual to consider this apart from brain. I have preferred to include all groups of nerve-cells of whatever kind under the one term, for several reasons. (1) It makes it easier for the general reader to conceive of the system as a whole, gradually evolved from the diffuse sensibility to vibration which characterises the single cell, through varying degrees of specialisation, to the more complex system (still capable of further evolu-

tion) which man possesses. (2) Though it is the general idea that knowledge of the external world comes only through the sense organs, it would seem possible that if the soul is in harmony with any life-force (definitions 2 and 5) such life-force should be able to communicate with it: to express such communication in terms of this life, the soul would then generate such vibrations as would influence the nerve centres of the brain concerned in stimulating thought or bodily movement of any kind (speech, writing, etc.).

11. **Mind.** It is customary to consider this as something at once more narrow, more abstract, and more vague (definition 2, note). There is however no particular advantage in confining mind to the limits of brain. The central nervous system depends upon stimuli from without for much of its activity, and the end organs of any sense are thus involved in mental processes. It is simpler to consider the mental unit to be composed of three parts, (1) the reception of the stimulating vibration, (2) its association with others or with their memories in the brain or elsewhere, (3) the generation of vibrations in response. For example, I feel a draught, I conclude that the open door is causing it, I get up and shut the door. Each of the three parts is a complicated process when considered in detail; it may be that the first

and last are more nervous and muscular in character than the second,—or that the second alone is entitled to be called a mental process. But the simpler classification is for all practical purposes sufficient. It must be remembered that a thought-unit in which the second or conscious reasoning process is suppressed or lacking (e.g. the mental parts of the action of walking), though it now may be classified under instinctive or reflex action must at one period have taken its place in the conscious mentality of the individual. According to this definition every activity of nerve cells which may give rise to thought is included as thought: this renders it easier to appreciate that influence of thought on bodily processes which is the basis of what is called Christian Science.

12. Memory. The physical basis of memory would appear to be intimately connected with that part of the nervous system concerned with association of stimuli. Some maps of the brain published by authorities on brain localisation[1] mark special regions for 'word memory,' 'music memory,' etc. If these are correct, it is impossible to conceive that each 'fact' is stored in a certain single cell, like honey in a comb, or books on a shelf, and pulled out when required. Some other theory must be evolved, as, for instance, that it is the nature of the

[1] See any textbook on Mental Disorders, Nervous Diseases, etc.

vibrations which we remember. This is at least comparable with the overtones in music, or the electric currents which surround a telegraph wire, i.e. it is based upon vibrations.

13. Personality. This is always a fluctuating quantity, varying from day to day and hour to hour. Insofar as it is physical or elemental it is closely bound up with the action of the nervous system, depending largely on habits of mind, on memory, and on general physical vitality. It is closely allied to if not even coextensive with ' temperament.' Insofar as it is spiritual, or of the soul, it depends for its manifestation through the body upon internal harmony. (Harmonising vibrations, Part I, Ch. III ; also definition 10, note.)

Fluctuations of personality are easily noted in children. In the study of any individual (of whatever age), it is more essential to have clearly in one's mind the tides of fluctuation normal to the individual than an abstract statement of what is considered the normal tide for the average even of ten thousand individuals. The problem not merely of education but of coexistence itself is one of individualisation.

Here belong police courts, assizes and prisons, in which the enquiry into tidal personality is held. In a community worthy of the name such inquiries would have taken place in school or at home, and

NOTES ON THE DEFINITIONS 77

their irregularities corrected by the establishment of internal harmony.

14. Will. Differing from desire, which is an habitual rate of vibration in certain parts of the nervous system tending to involve the whole in action: desire is a mixture of habit and craving. Only if directed by will is desire to be obeyed. Desire is elemental, will is spiritual.

    Here belongs passion as distinct from love (physical).

15. Growth. The increase in height and weight and the developing and ripening of the body I regard as no mere instinctive process, but as a definite and purposed activity of the life-form engaged in its own evolution. It would seem to possess a species of consciousness of a lower order than mental consciousness, perhaps an 'elemental' consciousness. It can at times manifest a fierce concentration which is exhausting to the individual and destructive of internal harmony: these times vary in incidence, and are by no means always, if at all, connected with the development of sex. It is a common error of a shallow psychology to ascribe to sex development all the manifestations of vitality in mind and body. The activities of growth and of nourishment in simpler life-forms, and in the more complex human being the activity of creative mental work, are at least equal, and frequently superior in influence upon

the individual to the elemental and unskilled labours of sex.
16. Community. The evolution of the community is considered later. It is sufficient here to call attention to the initial absurdity of the theory that the community may demand the death of the individual in order to secure its own permanence. It is an absurdity which strikes the common sense of the individual at once (Preface, p. 8, and Part IV, Ch. X). Only in a perverted or an ignorant mind can the co-existence of two be confused with the death of one. The causes of such confusion are examined later (Part III).
17. Authority. Not to be confused with 'an authority' (e.g. upon geology), but the claim which is made by 'the authorities.' (Compare 'competent military authority,' D.O.R.A. *passim.*)
18. Discipline. Or, the substitution of the will of one or more human beings for the internal harmony of another, as a means of control.
Here belong order, obedience, "the good of the community," and all other means used to secure the subjection of B to A in schools and elsewhere.
19. Punishment. Here belong fines, imprisonment, corporal and capital punishment, blockades, occupations and war.
20. Self-control. 'Generation of stimuli' includes action: e.g. the thought of saving life and the actions of jumping off a pier into

the sea, swimming, etc. 'Reception' includes inhibition of stimuli: e.g. in disregarding or refusing to hear advice to get out of the way in stopping a runaway horse.

21. Obedience. Voluntary obedience is in reality co-operation, and should not be termed obedience. Obedience to A against the will of B may be self-sacrifice: it may also be a sin (cf. Naaman, "When I bow myself in the house of Rimmon . . . .")

22, 23, 24. Instinct. Habit. Reflex action. These definitions are based on the theory that all nervous activity has at one period possessed the element of consciousness and will, and that this element may be dropped. (Definition 11, note.) Example: walking at the age of one or of eleven years. The voluntary character of involuntary acts may be redeveloped in certain circumstances: e.g. breathing, and many other movements usually regarded as beyond control.

25. Law. Not to be confused with 'natural law': e.g. law of gravitation, a statement which in the light of existing knowledge appears to be the best explanation of all facts of a certain kind: as soon as experience shows it to be incorrect it is discarded in favour of a new 'law.'

Moral law is the expression of established custom, and varies with the evolution of the community and with latitude and longitude.

There is no eternal law save that which

is of the spirit or soul (e.g. to love one's neighbour as oneself).

The Laws (e.g. Company Law, Military Law, Divorce Laws, etc.) are of their nature behind the times: they are of the past (e.g. Law as to Sunday Trading). They are temporary expedients. When one group in a community seeks to insist upon them in order to coerce another group, Authority and Discipline and Punishment are invoked. The flaw in the argument is that when coercion is used by A upon B, the A B community has ceased to exist and Law is then a contract which has lapsed and is no longer binding.

29. Attention. In addition to vibration among its contents, the cell has the property of changing the permeability of its membrane in some way. Example: the fertilised egg or cell changes the permeability of the external membrane so as to prevent the entrance of further fertilising agencies. It would seem possible that this property of cells may be connected intimately with the phenomenon of attention.

30. Latent period. Essentially an opportunity for self-control and its practice. When however A so influences the vibrations of B that B vibrates with an A harmony, then B will find himself unable to employ his latent period so as to harmonise with C, unless A so desires. A will not only control B's tendency but will have made it expressly to serve an A purpose.

SUMMARY OF PART II

IN everyday affairs it is essential to use words and phrases which are definite and clear. It is even more so when dealing with central theories and facts of human life, where misunderstanding may mean disaster. Words such as pain, memory, mind, fear, etc., have an added risk, since though each knows what they mean to himself he cannot assess their effect on others, and he also uses them without thought of analysis or definition. Vagueness of phrase, or ignorant, slovenly or deliberately perverse use of words makes possible the present tragic misconception of the community. Community means coexistence, a joint effort in every life-activity: its study is therefore a science of life, and must include something of most 'sciences': it must also pay due regard to religion, since this has a potent influence upon human nature. Any definitions of terms used in discussing life must be based directly upon the principles of life which underlie all existence. It is especially necessary to define the properties of the individual, if the community is to be clearly understood.

PART III

THE COMMUNITY
(i) EVOLUTION

CHAPTER VII

THE EVOLUTION OF THE COMMUNITY

Constituents of a simple cell 85
Reproduction by division 86
Simple coexistence of cells 88
Insect and animal communities 90

CHAPTER VIII

ANIMAL AND HUMAN COMMUNITIES

The argument from animal to human communities 94
Two forms of human community . . . 96
Iroquois and Western European 99

CHAPTER IX

THE GENERAL PRINCIPLES OF COEXISTENCE

A formula of coexistence 107
How to use the formula 107

Summary of Part III 111

CHAPTER VII

THE EVOLUTION OF THE COMMUNITY

CONSTITUENTS OF A SIMPLE CELL.

IN the simplest single cell it is possible to observe a definite limit at which it is separable from its surroundings : as we have said, to the ordinary man it has an inside and an outside. The inside apparently is not all of the same kind or form, not, so to speak, like a bottle absolutely full of oil, or a cylinder absolutely full of oxygen at the same pressure everywhere : it is as though several kinds of material in several forms were present in the protoplasm of the inside of the cell. There is a nucleus (a centre of activity), sometimes a nucleolus (a smaller edition of the nucleus), some apparently rod-like structures, and some small 'empty' spaces (or vacuoles). One may justly regard all these component parts as coexisting for common advantage : they form a simple community.

It is usual to draw a parallel between this state of affairs and the human communities of to-day, to deduce from the characteristics of the simpler the essentials of the more complex. To this there is no objection, *provided the analysis of the simpler be complete and all its essential characteristics stated.* The usual process is as follows. " The community is an organisation devised for the benefit of all its members, for the greatest good of the greatest number. Study a simple cell: note the interactivity of all its parts: see how it moves towards its goal by the common effort of its contents, how when one part changes its shape the others adapt themselves to it. Its life-force is centred in the nucleus: should this perish the whole cell perishes with it. What a lesson for us, how it teaches us to co-operate, so that each part serves all the others, and no one part is idle at the others' expense. How the whole groups itself around the nucleus, and how this distributes vitality throughout the whole. Let us beware how we may injure our community by selfishness, how we risk the welfare of the whole by independent action. Let no minority obstruct the rest, or interfere with the greatest good of the greatest number." Here is a semi-scientific basis for (1) an address to factory hands, (2) a recruiting speech, (3) a speech to scholars on Founder's Day, (4) a lecture on civics in a continuation school, (5) a sermon on cricket, (6) an address on Socialism or Bolshevism or Liberalism or Conservativism, (7) a 'conversation' between the chief members of a Supreme Council, (8) a speech in support of a Coalition Government or an Empire. And so on and so on. We have all heard it, and been partly convinced by it because it was partly scientific and partly based on a 'law of life.'

Reproduction by Division.

Let us examine the nucleus again. If the nucleus is injured the consequences to the existence of the

THE EVOLUTION OF THE COMMUNITY

cell might well be fatal. But suppose the nucleus be divided, what follows? Death? The division of the nucleus is one of the essential steps toward further life.[1] In the simplest cell, which reproduces itself by division, making two out of one, two attraction-bodies are formed. In due time the whole contents of the cell group themselves into two equally divided and definitely arranged colonies or associations, between which the envelope or external membrane folds itself into a dip, becoming a deeper fold which meets in the centre and ultimately isolates the two halves of the original cell, which then split off and form two separate cells. These then grow and mature, and in course of time and after a 'resting' period they divide again: presumably by their division they have become twice as many, and after their growth twice as strong. Through division these cells attain a kind of delegated immortality. But this part of the history of a cell would be most unsuitable for any of the eight purposes mentioned above, so—quite simply—it is omitted. Yet it would seem to be the natural process which all communities might imitate with safety. We may suppose the two attraction-bodies to be two policies, dividing a nucleus or committee or union or parliament equally or nearly so: what then occurs in our human communities to-day? If one part is by ever so little smaller than the other it is doomed to extinction: if both are equal, the chairman is called upon to give his casting vote,

[1] "The division of a cell is preceded by division of its nucleus" (Halliburton).

and the side which does not receive it is the smaller and is therefore cast out. So far have we departed from natural law in the political world.

There is another property of the cell which is almost universally disregarded when communities are considered, that is the constant vibration and movement of its component molecules, that movement which ceases only at death.

Simple Coexistence of Cells.

The subdivision of cells which are fertilised from without is essentially the same process as that of reproduction by division, only that the divided cells remain inside the original membrane. The contents of the fertilised egg divide and subdivide until there are sufficient cells to form the outer and inner (and later the middle) layers from which the various tissues of the body are formed. During this process the cells take the form imposed upon them by their position in relation to other cells: they specialise in their nature in order to fulfil their various functions, some forming bones, some muscles, the nerves, the lining of tubes and other cavities of the body, the hair and the skin. The completed human being is a conglomerate of millions of cells, specialised in function, interdependent for growth and vitality.

As with the simple cell, the human body is often taken as a type of the community, limbs, heart, lungs, etc., being regarded as images of the individual members of a state specialised in their occupations of miners, soldiers, bishops, members of parliament

THE EVOLUTION OF THE COMMUNITY

and the like. The parallel is true of the simple cell which reproduces by division and becomes 2, 4, 8, 16 and so on individuals: it is not true of the complex specialised conglomerate human being: *the human being is an individual, and an individual is not a community. Neither is a community an individual, but individuals.* There are two characteristics of community, a movement towards and a movement away, a breaking down and a building up: together they form that vibration of the community which is its life, which ceases with its death. It is the attempt to oppose this, to change the movement into a fixed state, which causes the fixation which is characteristic of death. It is then easy to understand why the attempt to imprison human life in what are known as States (the name is literally and metaphorically exact) produces not life but death: this is the initial error of thought which disintegrated the Empires of the past.

Where cells coexist in an individual with specialised functions they have not as a rule freedom of movement: they are obviously 'members of one body,' varying in relative importance. Man may remain man though shorn of many of his parts: some are vital, some not. There is only relative liberty of a restricted kind for his component parts, and each depends upon and ministers to the rest. It is however incorrect to suggest that these conditions are typical of community: as we have said, man is not a community but an individual. The general principles of combination in a life-form which becomes ever more complex, and of specialisation of function, are however common alike to individual and community: in analysing community, we shall be right if we compare and draw parallels between the general principles or laws which characterise both: we shall be wrong if we attempt to compare the special results of these principles in one with the special results produced in another. For instance, it is right—in comparing violin and piano—to say that both are vibration-producing machines which have strings; it would be wrong to say that because a piano has pedals the violin must also have them, or that the piano should always be played with a bow.

Insect and Animal Communities.

Since Solomon recommended a study of the ant, the theory of the human community has been largely based upon deductions from the habits and customs of bees, beavers, wolves and the like. If we model ourselves upon insects and animals we should at least make sure that we are justified in so doing. The various associations of animals are well and clearly classified by Lull.[1] He places them in two main groups, (1) associations of different species and (2) associations of the same species. Group (1) includes 'commensal' and 'symbiotic' life-forms. 'Commensal' is derived from two Latin words, *com* = *cum* = with or together with, and *mensa* = a table; so that a commensal association is one where the individuals of the

[1] *Organic Evolution*, Lull.

THE EVOLUTION OF THE COMMUNITY 91

community live with or on or in one another, and eat the same food. An example of this is the hermit crab and the hydroid envelope in which he lives. 'Symbiotic' is derived from two Greek words, *sun* = with and *bios* = life; so that in a symbiotic association the individuals forming the community are united in an organic or internal partnership so intimate as only to be severed by death. "It cannot exist between two animals, but only between an animal and a green chlorophyll-bearing plant,—or between a green and a colourless plant." Examples are a Green Hydra, and many Radiolaria. Group 1 includes two other forms of association,—viz. that of the beneficial bacteria and the higher animals, and that of harmful association between different species, i.e. Parasitism. The effect of parasitism on the 'host' is generally harmful, with no compensating benefit,—on the parasite it is almost invariably one of degenerative specialisation.[1]

Group 2 comprises Gregarious animals and Communal animals. 'Gregarious' (from a Latin word *grex* = a flock or herd) means those who herd together. 'Communal' is a development or evolution from gregarious. Lull says "it always implies division of labour, sometimes with physical differentiation, although in higher organisms increased intelligence may offset physical differences, the individuals being more adaptable to the various tasks of the community and not necessarily limited to one or two. True communalism is found in

---

[1] Lull's chapter on Parasitism and Degeneracy is full of interest for the student of sociology.

but two groups of organisms, the insects and mankind : in each instance the final culmination of a long and important evolutionary line." He places the ant community earlier in evolution than the human : of man he says : " He is to-day, especially in his more highly civilised state, the final product of communal life." The gregarious animals include wolves, buffaloes, beavers and pelicans : penguins are partly gregarious and partly communal, for, when the young in the nurseries are growing up and need more food, almost everyone turns out to get it for them except a few who are left to act as sentinels in charge—as it were—of the crèche. Bees, ants and man are the main examples of communal association (communists ?), their organisation varying not only from each other but among each species. These animal communities have one very important difference from their human competitors : their habitat is restricted by conditions of climate, vegetation and the like. The habitat of life in general on this earth may be conceived of as a very thin ball or sphere concentric with the earth and lying between the surfaces of contact of earth, water and air. It may be divided vertically or horizontally (compare a map of the Lake District, which gives not only area but in a corner a section of the country showing variations in height). Not only trees and shrubs but animals and insects as well choose the height most favourable to their continued existence, as well as the most suitable soil : their vertical environment is definitely marked. Horizontal environment is limited by temperature (which influences food) and by water supply, etc. The environment of special life-forms is thus still subject to the control of the three phases of elemental matter which characterise the world as a whole. The stork and the swallow (and of course countless other life-forms) secure extended advantages by migration: others are horizontally restricted in habitat. The position of the polar bears is bad enough in Regent's Park,— it is this enforced change of latitude as much as the imprisonment which renders them sterile or kills their offspring: life for them would be unendurable at the Equator. Man on the contrary has set himself free from his environment by the evolution of his brain: horizontally his limits are pushed back nearer and nearer to the Poles, though vertically he is still restricted to his original place by the needs of breathing.

CHAPTER VIII

ANIMAL AND HUMAN COMMUNITIES

THE ARGUMENT FROM ANIMAL TO HUMAN COMMUNITIES.

MARK TWAIN'S opinion of the ant [1] was that he was " a very overrated bird " : he goes so far as to say that an ant seems not to have enough sense to find his way home. Whether or no this be true, observation of the nearest colony of ants will demonstrate to anyone that his dispersed and wasteful expenditure of energy would be ill appreciated in a factory or a workshop. A far greater drawback to him as an example for mankind is that his community is based upon a slave population. The workers of the world may still obey the directions of Solomon with advantage, and become wise in the process. The following details should help them in their studies.[2]

White Ants. " Their social organisation has carried with it a remarkable physical differentiation. . . . The four castes are : First, the workers, small, blind, wingless, pale in colour. . . . Second, the soldiers : these are also blind and wingless and sexually undeveloped. . . . Third, the complemental males and females, also blind and wingless,

[1] *A Tramp Abroad*, Mark Twain.　　[2] *Organic Evolution*, Lull.

but with limited powers of procreation. . . . Their duty is to supplement the production of young in the event of failure on the part of the chief sexed individuals. The fourth caste are the true or chief males and females . . . being possessed of both wings and organs of vision, as they alone are concerned with the external world, all of the others being subterranean creatures which so far shun the light and air as to build covered tunnels for communication where burrowing is impracticable. . . . The young are all alike when first hatched, three moults being necessary to develope into large-headed individuals, and three more to form the latter into perfect soldiers."

There are Foraging and Marauding Ants: " the genus Eciton, the so-called driver ants, best illustrate this state of savagery, especially on the part of certain Brazilian species in which, in their long marches in search of booty, the great army is said to be marshalled by big-headed officers and led by scouts." Could anything be more illuminating? Perhaps this extract: " Slave-holding ants seem to be a natural outcome of the habit on the part of the marauding ants of bringing home the larvæ and pupæ of other ant-colonies. . . . Some slave-making ants are now absolutely dependent upon their captives for all work done in the colony, and one, Polyergus, has gone so far that it can neither dig nor care for its young or even keep itself from starvation in an abundantly stored nest without the aid of its slaves. Specialisation is leading Polyergus to its end."

The usual argument from such communities as

these to the human communities has some basis in fact, enough to make it misleading. The human community has its workers, small and pale in colour; it has its great army marshalled by big-headed officers and led by scouts: it is even developing a class which can neither dig nor care for its young or even keep itself from starvation without the aid of its slaves. Specialisation already begins to lead the modern polyergus (= hard-working ?) to his end. In our communities too the young are all alike when first hatched—as they were when Adam delved and Eve span. What differentiates us from the animals is that we do not like, and do not intend to continue, that system of specialising occupation and vocation which distorts the body and mind of its victims. We start from the fact that the young are all alike when hatched, and our evolution lies along the road of equality of opportunity toward the perfection of the individual.

Two Forms of Human Community.

"The Red Indians of Rupert's Land owned no manner of government or subordination. The father or head of the family obeyed no superior nor any command, and he himself only gave his advice or opinion. Consequently it was rarely that any great chief ever existed, and then only in time of war. It is true that when several families went to war, or to the factories to trade, they chose a leader, but to such a one obedience was only voluntary: everyone was at liberty to leave

ANIMAL AND HUMAN COMMUNITIES 97

when he pleased, and the notion of a commander was soon obliterated. Merit alone gave title to distinction ; such merit as an experienced hunter could boast, or one who possessed knowledge of communication between lakes and rivers, who could make long harangues, was a conjurer, or had a large family."[1] These were Red Indians in the service of the Hudson's Bay Company (1680–1700) : how they fared in contact with the communities of Western Europe may be read in these and other pages. They had still in their community the essentials of evolution, freedom of combination, voluntary co-operative action, the right to contract out, even their paternal authority giving only advice and opinion. Set against the background of a vast expanse of lake, river and forest, these wandering groups secured greater advantage for their individual members than the communities of France and England,—the France of Louis XIV with its splendour and squalor, the France which still infects the world with the same old dreams,— the England of the merchant adventurers and the press-gang. Those who wish to study the contemporary influence of these two communities upon their neighbours in Holland may do so in the thrilling pages of the history of William the Silent.[2]

About the same period (1600, or 1550–1650) there were many Red Indian community-forms of fluctuating character. " North and South, tribe was giving place to tribe, language to language : for the Indian, hopelessly unchanging in respect

---
[1] *The Great Company*, Willson, vol. i.
[2] *I Will Maintain*, Marjorie Bowen.

98 THE COMMUNITY : EVOLUTION

to individual and social development, was, as regards tribal relations and local haunts, mutable as the wind. In Canada and the northern section of the United States, the elements of change were especially active . . . while, in the region now forming the State of New York, a power was rising to a ferocious vitality, which, but for the presence of Europeans, would probably have subjected, absorbed, or exterminated every other Indian community east of the Mississippi and north of the Ohio."[1] These primitive communities were in a state of flux : it is as though the whole of North America were just at boiling-point, about to take shape in some larger unity. The tribal weapons were of the stone axe, spear and arrow-head type : their house utensils earthen pots and rush mats ; they knew rough picture writing with arbitrary signs having accepted meanings : they were inveterate smokers of the pipe. Their religion was what would now be termed grossly superstitious. They tattooed themselves and painted their bodies. They were ferociously cruel and extremely brave. " There was no individual ownership of land, but each family had for the time exclusive right to as much as it saw fit to cultivate." They dwelt in fortified ditched and palisaded towns. Their tents or huts had evolved into the Long House, a common dwelling for some twenty families, sometimes 200 feet long : one case is reported as measuring 180 yards from end to end. " Within, on both sides, were wide scaffolds, four feet from the floor, and extending the entire length of the

[1] *The Jesuits in North America*, Parkman. Macmillan, 1912.

house, like the seats of a colossal omnibus." The walls were a double row of saplings, bent inwards till they met and lashed together at the top: these were covered with large sheets of bark, overlapping like shingles, and—to keep all firm—covered with split poles lashed with bark-rope. All along the top an opening was left in the roof, to let in the light, and to let out the smoke from the fires which burnt lengthwise along the floor.

Iroquois and Western European.

Their communal experiment was never worked out: the story of the colonisation of America is the story of their destruction. It is useless to despise them or condemn: one may learn more by other means. Cruel they were, but so were men in Italy in 1400, in France in 1300. Their religion filled the trees and streams and hills and every animal with some strange god whom they feared and to whom they sacrificed. The Western European has found a new religion and a new idol, to whom if necessary the whole male population between eighteen and forty-five must give their lives. Debauched they may have been, but in a crude animal fashion which seems more natural than the refined perversions of ancient Greece or renascent Europe or those modern Babylons which reek of syphilis,—London, Berlin, Brussels, Paris, or any seaport town. Their long houses found successors in many camps in 1916, but ours were only for the braves, there were no children there, and women were kept for use elsewhere. Privacy was unknown:

there is little enough in many houses in this island to-day. Private ownership of land did not exist, each family tilling what they willed : were they better or worse than we, among whom one man may own 50,000 acres and another have to join a burial club to secure his plot of six by two ? Cruelty was an individual vice, and enemies were crucified or burnt or blinded or slowly cut in shreds : with us it is collective, and without the elemental decency of personal hate we spatter men in fragments, or disembowel them, choke, paralyse, blind and drive insane. They kept a rigid peace within their alliance : we have our League of Nations.

There seems no essential difference between the warlike and sacrificial customs of the Hurons and Iroquois, the Inquisition during the Spanish occupation of the Netherlands, and the Western European ethic which provided all the ghastly material for that library of medicine and surgery which was printed during the war to end war. We ended the Red Indian experiment, England and France : what have we made of ours ? Empire greater than Rome, a poisoned peace, the death of millions, and poverty, squalor and disease unparalleled in the history of the world. (Our own Government Report upon the influenza epidemic of 1918–1919 classes it as the second or third greatest plague of the world, matched only by the plague in the time of the Emperor Justinian and the Black Death.)

Two considerations are important in comparing the forms of human communities, one historical, one geological. Historical : it is necessary to take count of the length of known history of the race under discussion. Just as it is misleading to compare the elemental growth of a child of eleven and one of eighteen, it is mistaken to draw parallels between a 'community-experiment' recently begun and one which nears its final stage. Hurons might be compared with Zulus, England with Germany but not with Spain, and so on. Geological : it is very difficult to decide whether a community in a low stage of evolution is trying its experiment for the first time, or building again with the material of a vanished civilisation. The history of this globe has been so long, and the geological changes so vast, that something more than the mere military destruction of a single empire (as in the case of Mexico)[1] may have occurred. Whole countries may have been wiped out by some great cataclysm or the slow march of a glacial period, and the knowledge of man almost obliterated, to be painfully sown by a few survivors and even now only partially regained. In world-history, our present community is still a child in the womb, imperfect and awaiting birth. Yet, as the embryo shows the course of previous evolution, and one may trace it back to its earliest stage, so the present form of our coexistence holds in itself the secret of its origin, the essence of its vitality and the prophecy of its completion. To know what is essential, what atavistic, what further growth will see discarded, we have but to study the communities of the present in the light of the past, using our common sense as guide. The subject matter is within the reach of all : we need no special training in Imperial

[1] *Conquest of Mexico*, Prescott.

History, in civics or in the science of government, or the works of Marx or Machiavelli. We may watch the processes of coexistence at home, in the street, at the pictures, in trams and trains. Wherever two or three are gathered together is our laboratory. Who should know the essentials of community if not the man and woman in the street? Have they not been relying on community and co-operation for a million years? They have but one trap to avoid: let them discard the monkey and the other mammals, and use that organ which for ever differentiates them from the dog, wolf, horse, cat, sheep, deer, ox and ass, the birds and insects and the rest of the Noah's Ark,—which has set them free from the limitations of their environment. Let them stop delegating their responsibility, and use their brains before it is too late.

CHAPTER IX

THE GENERAL PRINCIPLES OF COEXISTENCE

" A COMMUNITY is the association of two or more human beings for common (though not of necessity identical or similar) purpose or advantage in their evolution" (definition 16).

A Community is an organism developed for the purpose of coexistence. As the original life-force acted upon the elemental material of the globe and caused it to express itself in form, so the life-force of individuals and the vitality of their elemental material act upon them and cause them to seek fuller expression in the form of a community. As the central essence of the individual is the soul (seeking further evolution in this life through and by means of the body), so the vital principle of the group of individuals forming a community is derived from the souls of its individual members. This must be true even in the humblest example of community (which may appear at first sight to be formed entirely for bodily advantage) : for bodily advantage, unless it be misused, is for the advantage of soul, since soul inhabits body for the primary purpose of soul-evolution. The evolution of body is at once an effect of the driving-power of soul, a labour-saving device, a means of increasing energy, and a re-agent upon the soul which caused it. During its existence every life-form is in a state of breaking down and building up: it changes constantly: it is not permanent: it may be termed the average of its own fluctuations: its existence is intimately connected with vibrations from within and from without which it constantly harmonises: it is always in movement: when movements and vibrations cease it dies. These things are true not only of the individual but of all his activities: they are especially true of his coexistence with others.

The vibrations which pervade all space and all matter, and cause particles and molecules to respond to their influence, are (in the case of communities) focussed through the individual members as 'individual vibrations': one may say that their wave-length is conditioned by the internal harmony of the individual. Individual vibrations call up a response from the members of a community whom they affect, just as vibrations in one group of nerve cells arouse others in other cells. It is this interchange of individual vibrations which constitutes the life of the community, as interchange of vibrations between thought-centres constitutes the life of the mind. And, as the vibrations of each individual must be governed by internal harmony, so the vibrations of the community must be harmonised. Insofar as individual vibrations in a community neutralise each other the community ceases to exist.

Communities, like individuals, may reproduce themselves by fertilisation, or by division: like

GENERAL PRINCIPLES OF COEXISTENCE 105

individuals they change; they may suffer from disease; they have an eternal quality which survives as a part of race experience.

As with the individual, there are three phases of community: a lower, which is bodily; a higher, which is of the mind; the highest is of the soul. The various communities of insects and animals (p. 90) are bodily or elemental in character. Those of the mind are higher in the scale of evolution: here belong all human communities. Though higher than those which are merely bodily, they are not yet far evolved, and the principles which underlie their formation and govern their activities have been little studied. Those of the soul, and these too are less evolved than they might be, are to be found between individual followers of God. They are as a rule confused with those great organisations of belief which aim at permanence, and thus violate the condition of life, which is change. These latter resemble the ruined temples of Egypt or those great cathedrals of Europe which are national monuments rather than homes of faith. Those who would study a community of the soul should rather observe the efforts made on behalf of the starving children of Europe by individuals of all nations in 1919-1921.

The highest form of community of soul is that between the individual and God.

All three phases of community shade into each other, and there is no hard-and-fast line between them; yet in general there is little difficulty in deciding to which phase a community belongs. It may indeed pass from one phase to another and its essential character change. A good example of all this may be found in the coexistence of two individuals of opposite sex. In the case of two animals, the purpose of coexistence is the more elemental one of reproduction. With human beings this may also be the central purpose; if so, the community is elemental. Should the purpose be not reproduction but the process of fertilisation only, the community may be of even a lower order. (Coexistence for this purpose where one individual is bought, e.g. in a *mariage de convenance*, may be termed financial or economic: it is in no sense a community of love). A union based chiefly on the elemental phase is secure only so long as 'passion' lasts: this failure to distinguish between lower and higher is a frequent source of disaster in countries where law regards such unions as permanent. Coexistence based on the lower phase and on mutual intellectual attraction may vary from lower to higher and grow ultimately into either. Where intellect and soul both influence the choice, the community is of a still higher order, and is but reinforced by the vibrations of the more elemental attributes of man. A community may remain of this order even though physical coexistence become impossible, or one of the individuals should die: it may continue to exist as a community in the higher phase, manifesting itself as such through the eternal attribute of humanity, the soul. Only where soul is a part of sexual or other coexistence can a community hope to be permanent: the source of error lies in the confusion of phase and the mistaking of a lower for a higher phase or vice versa.

GENERAL PRINCIPLES OF COEXISTENCE

A Formula of Coexistence.

Let A and B be two individuals (or groups) composing a community: A and B then coexist for the purpose of similar or identical or different advantage. Should this purpose cease to be served by their coexistence, the community AB is at an end.

NOTE.—The formula may be called dangerous or destructive, a negation of life or an incitement to licence; it may be said that without permanence of community there is no individual security, that if this were our basis of life we should sacrifice law and order, or the sanctity of marriage, or even the hope of human progress, to say nothing of international alliances, the Empire or the United Kingdom. Its ignorant or unreasoning application would no doubt produce such results, just as the present diseased and perverted theory of community has done, is doing and always must do. The modern erection of false community into a God and the doctrine of human sacrifice to it which is widely held, has devastated Europe and diverted the course of evolution. The objection to the formula is because it destroys the present theory of community, and those who gain by that theory stand to lose by change. There are however more who stand to gain by change, though to make just any change rather than endure the old may well prove fatal. The formula will stand the test of experiment because it is based on general principles which underlie all forms of life. A similar objection might be made to razors, because they are sharp, or cut deep, or because men kill their wives or children or one another with them, or negroes throw them with deadly effect. Yet men make them still, and most use them with common sense.

How to Use the Formula.

When applying the formula in the analysis of a community, several considerations have to be taken into account.

1. Where A and B are groups, their number is not fixed and unchanging. Community implies a breaking down and building up: this is common to all activities of life. A or B may lose members by death, by resignation of membership, by filtration from A to B or vice versa.

2. A and B may not be the only groups: C may be a member, or indeed the whole of the rest of the alphabet may be included. This should not be forgotten, though for the sake of simplicity we may confine ourselves to as few letters as possible.

3. The community AB, formed for one purpose, may be found to serve another equally well: it will still however remain an AB community, though for the second purpose A and B may so interchange as to be apparently quite other in character, or A or B may dwindle almost to nothing through filtration.

4. Individuals in either A or B may be members of communities other than AB: should the purpose most important to them appear to lie in CD or XY rather than in AB, they will naturally absent themselves from AB for a period or to some extent, or even leave it altogether.

5. It may happen that the purpose of AB may not be served for either A or B, and yet both may prefer to remain AB through considerations of general or other advantage.

6. When A finds its purpose served, and B finds its purpose not served or even definitely hindered by the continuance of AB,

    (i) B may remain in AB for other advantage.

GENERAL PRINCIPLES OF COEXISTENCE 109

(ii) B may desire to leave AB, and be prevented by A. The community AB has in essence then ceased to exist, and the attempt to render it permanent in opposition to the wishes of B produces a state of disease, the symptoms of which are in an appeal to authority, law, precedent or force,— in B resistance to A, with A's symptoms : B is infected with A's disease. The health of both A and B can be secured only by division : they then will be able to recombine with other groups and form other communities. In an enforced continuance of AB in a state of disease, either A may kill B, or B may kill A, or both may die. In any case the disease may infect the other communities to which individuals from A or B belong.

Simple and striking examples of all but the last of these may be found in the history of Parliament. The common purpose is, in theory, government. (See Ch. XI.) (1) There is considerable filtration from the Labour Party to the Conservatives. (3) The first clause is applicable to the history of many election mandates. (4) One man may apply for the Chiltern Hundreds for private reasons : another may find the cause of his nationality better served by refusing to take his seat at Westminster at all. (5) This explains the apparent anomalies of many Party votes.

(6 i) B, an individual member, may remain in his Party for advantages which he

considers possible in the future, e.g. office or a title. This however implies that his membership of AB was not primarily for the purpose of governing: it is rather a case of dissimilar or double advantage.

(6 ii) For examples of this, one cannot do better than leave the history of Parliament and study that of the American War of Independence, or the coexistence of England and Ireland. The latter is the classical instance of the infection of other communities to which the members of A and B may belong.

Other difficulties of detail may at first sight seem to show that the formula is inaccurate, but a careful analysis will as a rule prove that it is correct. It cannot be too strongly insisted upon that when community ceases to exist the whole history of life upon earth calls aloud for the separation of A and B. This is the only way to secure their recombination in other communities (or even in a renewed AB), and that freedom of experiment upon which their further evolution depends. No life-form can continue to exist without freedom of movement, and in a state of discord which renders internal harmony impossible. Disregard of this fundamental truth has turned our 'civilised' communities into bridge-heads, occupied districts, famine areas, plague spots, and the whole crazy patchwork of an incompetent statesmanship ignorant of the first principles of coexistence.

SUMMARY OF PART III

OBSERVATION of a simple cell shows its principal constituents. When drawing a parallel between cell and community, it is usual to omit those constituents and functions which would interfere with the parallel: as for example the process of reproduction by division. The present-day custom of dividing communities into majority and minority is opposed to the principles of coexistence. The parallel between the component parts of a human being and the members of a community is only partially true: for a human being is not a community but an individual. It is not permissible to compare the special features of a certain lifeform and those of the community of which it is a member, but only to compare the general principles which underlie both. The parallels customarily drawn between insect or animal and human communities are false, since man differs in an essential property from the animals: his mental evolution has set him free from his environment.

In comparing two communities it is necessary to take into account their stage of evolution, grouping primitive with primitive, and so on. One may however attempt to gauge the progress of evolution by comparing the primitive with the more evolved.

The general principles of coexistence are the same as those which underlie all life. Communities, like the original material of the earth, may be grouped into three phases, a lower, a higher and a highest : these shade into each other in varying degrees.

The analysis of community is made easier by employing a formula, a general statement applicable to all instances of coexistence.

PART IV

THE COMMUNITY
(ii) ORGANISATION

CHAPTER X

THE NATURAL CONTROLS OF COEXISTENCE

	PAGE
Common sense	116
Sympathy	117
Tact	118
Self-reliance	118
The stimulus of creative work	119
The principle of voluntary association	120
An instance of the use of natural controls	121

CHAPTER XI

AN INDIVIDUAL AND HIS COMMUNITIES

Home	123
Street	124
Bus	124
Ticket-office	125
Train	125
Work	126
Fire-engine	126
Lunch	127
Mental community	128

CHAPTER XII

THE COMMUNITY OF SCHOOL

Lines of cleavage	132
Relations between its members	132
Child life	134
Authority	136
When school is a community	139
What school really is	140
Summary of Part IV	142

CHAPTER X

THE NATURAL CONTROLS OF COEXISTENCE

It is literally true that to-day " The Community " has become an object of almost religious worship, and that Church and State combine to condemn any and every suggestion of change. It is intelligible that those who would lose by such change should resist it: it is harder to understand why those who might gain should continue to support a form of coexistence which obviously fails to secure them even the most elementary decencies and comforts. They are however influenced by the experiences of their childhood, in which they have been taught to believe in the moral necessity of punishment, the duty of disciplined obedience to authority, and the sanctity of law: they are thus the more ready to reject any theory which may bring them into personal contact with the system of fines and imprisonments by which the present form of community is maintained. The cry that the State is in danger is enough by itself to stampede group B in any direction desired by A.

Yet neither fear nor law secured community of effort in the past. There are natural controls more fundamentally engrained in human nature than any legal sanction, controls evolved by the daily needs of life. Amongst them are the internal harmony which is manifested in self-control, and the common sense by which men govern their transactions and activities.

Common Sense.

We have seen how for ages the higher animals and man have practised combination and the formation of communities as a means to further evolution. This habit of mutual aid and co-operation for common purposes produced a whole technique of coexistence, ahead of law because it was constantly being adapted to present needs, and gaining in flexibility because it was not written down. Mutual aid does not depend upon compulsion or fear: it is the outcome of voluntary co-operation for common advantage. Co-operation implies a friendly give and take, comparable to that mutual change of outline which occurs when cells are combined in groups (e.g. in the earlier formations of living tissue which mark the development of the fertilised ovum, or in the space-saving design of honeycomb in hexagonal form). Yet it is more than this, for it springs from the interplay of living forces and becomes that combination of individual harmonies which is the common chord of coexistence. Co-operation implies mutual trust: there is no individual security in coexistence with one whom you expect to fail you at a pinch. The age-long custom of common effort and the technique it evolved is embodied in what is, very literally, common sense, common feeling: it implies appreciation of the needs of others, a proper use of the latent period, and the will to attain common action. Such habits—if capable of being transmitted to offspring—must long ago have become inherited characteristics of mankind: if not, then they are acquired in the very earliest stages of infancy, at the period when the child is perfecting individual movement.

The technique of common sense produces neighbourliness, such deep-seated customs as the rule of the road, or the voluntary formation of a queue at a ticket-office: it is the confidence in the honesty of the other man which—in spite of frequent shocks—remains the basis of commerce and finance: it is that reliance upon passers-by which makes it possible for a blind man to cross Piccadilly Circus, or for a stranger in a district to ask the way of one he has never met before. It is the heaped-up experience of ages of evolution, and the instinctive resort of the human being confronted by a new environment: it will survive when policemen and magistrates and the Lord Chief Justice and the Courts of Appeal have ceased to function.

SYMPATHY.

This is essentially a natural control. The original Greek word, *sumpatheia*, is made from *sun* (= with) and a stem *path* (= feel), and is translated by Liddell and Scott as " fellow-feeling, community of feeling, sympathy." According to them the radical sense of the stem of the word (*path*) is " to receive an impression from without." This, as we have seen, is to receive vibrations by the senses. What more potent instigation to common action could be imagined than for A and B to receive the same vibrations, and by means of their individual internal harmony to secure the most efficient co-operation in their response? Not only in its literal meaning but in very deed is sympathy identical with common sense.

TACT.

This is no more than the outward sign of sympathy: it is the touch which plays so important a part in the technique of music (the production of harmonious vibrations). Used in a more abstract sense, it is in German the 'beat' which secures rhythm: with us it implies that appreciation of the moods or potentiality of another which enables us to secure his fullest response. It is an outward symptom of that effective reception and generation of vibrations which is of the very nature of man, —it is in the fullest sense a natural control of coexistence.

SELF-RELIANCE.

In spite of the injurious effects which dependence on external authority has had upon the human organism, this still remains a vital characteristic of man. It is a product of common sense, internal harmony and external stimuli. Since life presents the data upon which we must act (and must abide by the results of our action) in no ordered progression, the hard-and-fast rule of precedent becomes an impossibility. Among the whirl of stimuli we have to choose, to react to this, to inhibit that, and our most certain guide is that force within each of us which has driven us to evolve from the simpler forms of life. To attain its maximum effect, practice in free experiment and self-reliance should be given to man from the earliest stages of his being.

The Stimulus of Creative Work.

This is one of the most vital needs of existence: creative work provides mankind with the fullest opportunities of self-expression (the generation of vibrations): it is essential to his evolution. The recognition of this truth is the basis of later educational reform. Unfortunately, the curriculum of the ordinary school combines with the economic slavery of the adult to render opportunities of creative work which shall be in harmony with the individual increasingly difficult to secure. The child must pass its Standards, and the man or woman take the first job that presents itself— or starve. 'Vocational' schools will not remedy this; they merely lessen the chance of starvation. It is not credible that a human being free to choose would spend a lifetime at a typewriting machine or in an office.

Should proof be needed that creative work is a natural activity of mankind, all that is necessary is to study the effects of occupationless confinement. The past history of prisons will furnish countless cases, with their inevitable symptoms of mental and physical ruin. The perversion of this natural need through economic conditions is one of the most serious consequences of an industrial 'civilisation.' Given opportunity for such work and freedom of experiment in it, the human mind progresses in a way which is otherwise impossible.

The Principle of Voluntary Association.

When A and B no longer join in common purpose and community of effort ceases, the natural course is for them to separate and recombine with C or D or even with B or A upon another basis. It is unnatural that A should compel B: it is natural that they should both be free: vibrations imposed from without destroy internal harmony. The common sense of human beings readily recognises the truth of this. What is more striking is that even repressive legislation is in a way based upon this principle. Such is the conviction of A that B believes in and will have freedom, that laws passed by A expressly for the coercion of B must somehow be given the appearance of B's consent.[1] This is the one method of ensuring that modern democracies will continue to tolerate their own bondage: only in this way could an Englishman who believed that a man's house is his castle be brought to acquiesce in the restrictions imposed upon his

[1] This underlies the theory and practice of plebiscites.

NATURAL CONTROLS OF COEXISTENCE

life by 'Dora.'[1] His conviction that freedom is his natural state still remains, and will reassert itself. For he knows that the principle of voluntary association is essential to his evolution.

AN INSTANCE OF THE USE OF NATURAL CONTROLS.

Common Sense, Sympathy, Tact, Self-reliance, the Stimulus of Creative Work, the Principle of Voluntary Association, these and forces such as these are the natural controls of human coexistence. But since Authority refuses to recognise them, we are driven to suppose an instance in which for once they replaced the usual instruments of government.

Imagine Western Europe devastated by the most awful war in the history of the world,—its Empires crumbling, the boundaries of its States obliterated, its industries ruined, its finance destroyed, its peoples starving and diseased, its hospitals and asylums full to overflowing, its streets crowded with maimed and halt and blind and unemployed, its very earth and air impregnated with infection and decay. Imagine a group of men assembled at Versailles to plan a community in which the survivors might coexist. In your imagination dower the conference with the common sense of a mother, the sympathy of a father, the tact of an old nurse, the self-reliance of a boy or girl: imagine them inspired with a will to creative work, convinced of the principle of voluntary

[1] The Defence of the Realm Act.

association, and possessed of an internal harmony, vibrating in response to the eternal life-force. Such simple natural controls would have enabled them to do their work successfully.

Instead of common sense they clung to precedent—precedent in the midst of undreamed disaster: instead of sympathy they felt distrust: they substituted force for tact. Instead of self-reliance they were inspired by fear—fear when the whole world looked to them for courage. The stimulus of creative work found no response in policy: they buried life afresh under the weight of empire. Instead of voluntary association they chose dismemberment. They failed, because of Authority, and Law, and Punishment, the creaking engines of Compulsion and the whole vast majesty of Force. Cynicism they knew, and sleek opportunism, and the half-convinced assertions of the doctrinaire, but coexistence was beyond their grasp. No mere deliberate wickedness could have caused such failure: it required a monumental ignorance of life to frame the peace which ended peace.

CHAPTER XI

AN INDIVIDUAL AND HIS COMMUNITIES

EXAMPLES of coexistence are always within reach. There is no need for laboratory experiments or apparatus. Anyone may study the subject on his way to work, with no further guides than his own common sense and his own internal harmony. In one working day, from the time he gets up until he goes to bed, a man may often test the theory of coexistence and apply the formula. If either seem to be true, the result will be the more convincing because it will have been true of ordinary occurrences of daily life, the popular and practical things which everyone knows. Here are some of the communities to which a business-man may belong in a day.

Home community.—Husband, wife, children, servant are its members. Common purposes between husband, wife and children, (1) elemental existence, (2) family life. The parents also form an inner community of their own.

Common purpose of family and servant, elemental existence. Separate purpose of servant, economic security. Before and at breakfast internal harmony may be at a discount, and the harmony of the community impaired. After breakfast father goes to business and the children to school: mother and servant form a community for housework. Non-resident members of the community, postman, milkboy, etc.

Out in the street on the way to the bus, father becomes a member of what is virtually a community for the purpose of going. He adapts his movements to the traffic he meets, keeps the rule of the road, greets his friends, and so on. Chaotic vibration and movement become controlled. The common purpose of a street-community is movement. Individuals constantly traverse each other's path, going to a shop, crossing the road, etc.: each avoids collisions by varying his movements. The membership of the movement-community of the street is constantly changing, as people start or reach their destination. After a few minutes father takes a bus to the station, as he was late in finishing breakfast.

The bus contains a community of a most interesting type, with fluctuating membership and varying purposes. No one wishes to go exactly the full journey: not even the driver and guard stay with the machine at the end of its day, in the garage. Few would choose the fixed route if a shorter were available: it is merely the average of the needs of all who travel in the bus, some to a counter in a shop, some to a station, others to a house in a road near by, others to the terminus and then further. Everyone goes part of the way, and for no one does the bus go the whole way: when common advantage is no longer served, the individuals get out, and recombine in other

AN INDIVIDUAL AND HIS COMMUNITIES 125

communities. Membership of the bus-community is entirely voluntary; one can imagine what father's conduct would be if the guard—as representing authority—insisted on his becoming a life-member.

Having reached the station, he gets out, and—not having renewed his contract—goes to buy a ticket. Here he harmonises his movements in the new environment of a queue: the members of the ticket-community form up in a line one behind the other and maintain their internal harmony as best they may:—their ability to do this depends on their stage of evolution. The harmonised vibrations of the individuals in the line are strong enough to influence those who might attempt to go out of their turn. The basis of this combined action is common purpose, and the control is the natural one of common sense. The queue is often quoted as an example of government by authority, whereas it is nothing of the kind: it is an example of the failure of another community (the shareholders) to provide enough windows to the ticket-office.

In the train is another going-community, where the conditions resemble those of the bus. Let us apply the doctrine of the sanctity of the community and the sacrifice of the individual to father and his friends in their usual compartment. Shall we send a company's official to persuade them to do their duty to the utmost, and stay with the train to the bitter end—even though it means all the way from Euston to Aberdeen—for the good of the shareholders? Father is a shareholder, yet he will refuse to go past his station, because his train-community exists only so long as it serves his purpose: as for his shares, he can withdraw them when he wishes. In everyday practical instances the sanctity of the community and the perils of its division are merely unconvincing: it is only when complexity or other factors blur the issue that such theories are tolerated for a moment and common sense is deceived.

At the office father settles down to work, doing his bit of the widespread and complicated business of the cotton trade. His community now reaches from one side of the Atlantic to the other. His firm specialises in prints which have a particular attraction for 'natives' in many lands: from the plantation to Wall Street, through Liverpool and Manchester, down to the docks again and out to sea, and up some mosquito-ridden creek in West Africa, you will find members of his cotton-community everywhere. There are others in Egypt and India and South America. It is a closer community than that of the bus or train, and not so easily left or joined: but no compulsion by external authority forces father to stay in it till the end of his days, or makes the firm keep him when common or individual advantage is no longer served.

On the way to lunch he joins the street-community for the purpose of going: it is crowded, complex, and characterised by movement and life. Suddenly a fire-engine is heard, its alarm insistent and menacing: the thoughts of those who listen recombine with amazing swiftness into fire-complexes: the movements in the street alter: the going-community dissolves and recombines in fresh formations at this new stimulus. The rule of the road is kept, or broken if necessary, as carts and wagons get out of the way with incredible speed into impossible places: a clear space opens through the traffic, and the engine passes through a community organised of itself for the purpose of saving property or life. When it is gone, the street community recombines. The controls are common sense, sympathy, voluntary association, and those other natural forces: where a policeman helps, it is because his position on point duty enables him to see traffic better, and because the very reason for his existence is the co-ordination and harmonising of the vibrations of the community.

Lunch is the common purpose of a fresh community, resembling breakfast. Over coffee afterwards in the smoking-room father joins a group of friends for conversation or a game: one more community. Then back through the street to the office (and America and India and the other places), the train, bus, street and home. The evening is spent in further changes, with mother and the children[1] and friends who come to call,—new groupings, fresh purposes, free associations. And so to bed.

There are other group-activities which influence the crowded day,—international communities of trade, or of the employés (trade unions), or the

[1] For a detailed analysis of the children's community of school and its purposes, see Ch. XII.

employers.[1] Life is an interwoven throbbing complexity of effort, constantly changing in its manifestations, always new,—yet always subject to the laws of coexistence. Co-operative effort as the means to further evolution is but the life-form in which associated individuals respond to the force which underlies all life.

Mental Communities.

When father reads a book before he goes to bed, he presents a striking example of mental community which well repays detailed analysis. " Because of his intelligence and communal co-operation man is no longer subject to the laws which govern the adaptation of animals to their environment. . . . His future evolution, in so far as it is progressive, will be mental and spiritual rather than physical."[2] Now mental evolution is an affair of brain, and brain is an organ individual in its activities which it is impossible to confine within the limits of a herd or pack. With it man can abolish time and space ; he can examine the constituent elements of the stars, or visualise the masses of earth and water on this globe a million years ago, or guess with a fair certainty the kind of rock to be found a thousand feet below his house. He may reside in England and yet live mentally in Italy or ancient Egypt. Like a certain dear old bishop, his body may be in the nineteenth century, his head in the seventeenth,

[1] Compare the Federation of British Industries.
[2] *Organic Evolution*, Lull.

AN INDIVIDUAL AND HIS COMMUNITIES

and his heart in heaven. Or, like Lord Haldane, his spiritual home may be in Germany. The mental community to which he belongs is one which he may join or leave at will, and it may be anywhere in the world, or everywhere, in past, present or future: often it will be more like life as he wishes it were than as it is. So he sits and reads, and for a time his usual environment is forgotten and he moves in another world.

The formation of mental communities occurs regardless of the limits of language or country. They may be racial, as for instance where Jews all the world over are interested in the later politics of Palestine; in this case the physical and the mental are both involved. They may be entirely unconnected with race or country in purpose, as in that select community to which the researches of Professor Einstein are intelligible, or in the wider yet equally international group of chess-players who are interested in the achievements of Capablanca. They may appear at first to be narrowly national, like that which centres round the *Morning Post*, or as obviously international as that of the Communists or the International Workers of the World, or apparently international like the present League of Nations.

The races of mankind are classified according to (1) their shape of skull, (2) their kind of hair, so that one is known as round-headed and curly-haired, another as long-headed and lank-haired, and so on. The earlier human communities may be grouped as tribal or nomad or monarchic, from their social or political organisation. The communities into which civilised peoples fall to-day show three main classes, the governing, the governed and the 'professional' class or 'intelligentsia.' The latter is a middle group of somewhat vague outline and recent development: it would be fair to consider it the more mentally evolved of the three, but it is still unstable, and tends to recombine about the other two as nuclei. To one or other of the three father may be expected to belong, and there will be a far closer connection, a more potent common purpose and advantage, between him and the individuals of his group in other countries than between him and a member of another group in his own country. For instance, if he is a member of the governing class here, he will have more in common with the governing class in America or France or even Germany than he has with the servant who will make his breakfast to-morrow. Let us leave him to read in peace, an adherent of the governing class, pondering over the sanctity of the community and the dangers of change. Or, if he is a "worker," let us imagine him trying to make ends meet, or thinking about the merits of a political strike as a means to adapting the community to his own requirements. The time will come when he will study the many communities to which he has belonged during the day, and be by that so much the nearer to the solution of the problem of government.

CHAPTER XII

THE COMMUNITY OF SCHOOL [1]

IN analysing the community of school it is well to remember not only the formula of coexistence (Ch. IX) but also the definition of education (Ch. V) as " the provision of conditions suitable to further evolution." There are two forces to consider, (1) the desire to model the school upon the generally accepted idea of community, (2) the will to base its organisation upon human needs. Keeping these factors in mind, we may now proceed to examine our material, simplifying the process at the outset by choosing a boarding school in the country. It is more isolated, and shows the essential features of the organism all the more clearly because it is so.

Membership of this community includes all who have common advantage in it : we should therefore consider not only children but also Staff, parents, servants and those who work about the estate, bring food or supply material, etc. It is widespread in its extent : we may however

---

[1] Whilst it is plainly impossible to forget what one has learned from the places in which one has worked, I have done my best to write of school in general and not schools in particular. It would be incorrect to take this chapter as applying to any special case,—it is an analysis of school and not of a school.

omit the outlying individuals wherever possible, and make the problem still simpler by concerning ourselves chiefly with servants, children, Staff and Head.

Lines of Cleavage.

At the outset one is struck by the rigid social system of school. The servants are on a lower plane, a kind of slave population: the majority of the children form a 'fourth estate,'—the monitors, prefects and the like are a House of Commons, the Staff a House of Lords. On the top of the pyramid is seated the Head (a King or Queen), from whose mouth as in a mediæval picture there issues a scroll bearing the school motto, or the words ' L'état, c'est moi ! "

The Relations between its Members.

The relations between the four estates and the servants are very clearly defined. In most schools there is a local name for the latter: the children call them 'slavey' or 'skivvy' or 'grocer,' or some other name implying inferiority in social status. It is almost unheard-of to find servants attending the classes in their spare time.

Among the children there is a line of division between those who are governed and those who govern: office-holders such as head boy or girl or the captain of the first eleven are above the level of ordinary prefects or monitors, and these again are above the fourth estate. It is quite usual for younger children to hesitate to speak to older ones unless first spoken to; there are, of course, in every school countless things an older child may and a younger may not do, e.g. wearing long or short trousers, a coat collar turned up or down, etc.

There is a distinct line of cleavage between children and Staff, depending partly upon age (this would appear to be quite natural or elemental) but principally upon authority (see definition 17, and note 17, Ch. VI. It appears in even the most trivial conversation, where the child says 'sir' and the member of the Staff omits the corresponding politeness. When Staff and children are working together in class it is even more marked, and may in extreme cases effectively insulate each from the vibrations of the other. To some extent fear is a factor in the problem, because authority implies obedience and disobedience punishment, and punishment fear. There is also a fear of Staff for children, though this is frequently denied. Yet new, young, or ineffective teachers fear lest their classes become troublesome or noisy, with a reputation for indiscipline which may react on themselves and cause their dismissal: there is sometimes a very real economic servitude of Staff to children.

This fear enters largely into the relations of Staff to Head: there is also between them a definite atmosphere of privilege, of social position, or of caste, which must be considered even though it is hard to define. In some schools members of the Staff cultivate an attitude to the Head not essentially different to that which a child exhibits to the Staff by saying "sir," or "teacher," etc.

This may be described as an artificial respect rather than a human relationship. (Its absence is noted at once, though its presence is taken for granted and usually ignored. For instance, in calling over a class on an insufferably hot day, many would be shocked into activity by the following answer: " Brown ? " " Here." " Jones ? " " Here." " Smith ? " " Here." " Robinson ? " " Here." " Ashton ? " A sleepy voice as of a bored acquaintance telephoning from a distance replies " Hel-lo." One might produce the same effect by saying to the Head, " But, my dear man, it isn't good enough ! ")

In some schools there still exists a ' subject ' caste. This is an extremely interesting specimen of cleavage, in which Classics is separated from Science, and those who teach either consider Handwork as a rather menial occupation. As for Art, it is often regarded as not a subject at all, but a toy, or something like a beautiful bird in a cage kept to amuse the children or to impress visitors. The domestic Staff, i.e. Matron or Housekeeper, comes somewhere between the teaching Staff and the servants.

From this arrangement of social strata it follows that the child is well separated from the Head : this is usually considered desirable, since it enables the authority which rests in him or her to radiate throughout the whole with greater efficiency.

Child-life.

This is the life-force of the community of school : it would pay those who have to deal with it to look back every now and then and try to visualise what it needs and whence it comes. It is a long way from a spiral nebula to school, past simple cell and the more complex organisms, past the communities of animal or insect or early man, along the endless corridors of evolution and round the corners of heredity, until the individual reaches the door of your classroom, walks in and sits down as a member of your lesson-community. Unkempt or nicely dressed, obedient or troublesome, clever, stupid or just ordinary in its abilities, it is a bigger thing than even the State System of Education which now conditions its environment. At first the product of eternal vibrations acting upon the three-phase material of the world, it has evolved itself by countless experimental combinations with more complex groups, by myriad attempts at adaptation and improvement, gradually developing its inheritance through the medium of its environment. It has strewn its nursery, the earth, with countless discarded shapes and skeletons, struggling desperately to survive vast changes, clinging tenaciously to the contact-horizons of earth, air and water amid the submergings and upheavals of great continents. Here was no rigid childhood's time-table, but an ever-changing series of fresh combination, of dissolution, of movement conditioned by the activities of others, culminating at last in man. Man, characterised in every fibre of his being and every manifestation of his vitality by that movement and change which gave him birth and rendered evolution possible, and by that engrained habit of co-operation and mutual aid upon which he now instinctively relies for further progress,—this is the individual who now forms part of the community of school, this life-form striving toward internal harmony, quivering in response to stimuli, throbbing with self-generated vibrations, craving fresh opportunities of free experiment. This is the life which knocks at your door, comes in and sits, to wait for your co-operation. This is the force which ultimately will adapt the school community to its needs.

Authority.

When the door is shut and teacher and taught are in their places, the room encloses a community : individual harmonies must then be tuned so that the community may have its internal harmony —the condition essential to the best receiving and generating of vibrations (Ch. III) : this is obtained by the use of the natural controls (Ch. X). The beginning of every lesson is an example of the technique of coexistence, the rest of it is a further practice of the same : the whole is but another experiment in evolution for both teacher and taught. *The relation between those who teach and those who learn is that of Co-operative Mentality.* From all that has been said as to the harmonising of vibrations it follows that each individual is ultimately responsible for his own control : he must also be given freedom of further experiment. These are the principles which underlie all later educational reform, though up to the present they are not absolutely accepted even in those experimental schools which are said to base their practice upon them. Sooner or later the forces of child-life will secure their acceptance in every school.

Co-operative mentality and authority cannot coexist as bases of control: they are mutually exclusive. It may at first seem strange that authority should exist at all, seeing that external interference is opposed to the real development of internal harmony; but not more than one in a thousand teachers will agree that it is an evil. In fact, the school community as generally organised may be compared to reinforced concrete, in which the particles of cement are children and Staff, and the iron rods or wires are the rules and regulations of Authority, put there to hold all together under any strain. We shall see later that authority in school is one of the strongest bonds by which group A controls group B.

Authority is " the claim of one human being to control another." No claim is made more frequently, or is more diametrically opposed to every principle of coexistence. That it is still made in schools and even extolled as the basis of discipline is largely due to two errors: (1) most people, even educational reformers, confuse what seems and what is; (2) many people desire to confuse what seems and what is. These two groups will repay detailed examination.

(1) This error is inherent in the human mind, hence it is unfair to blame an earnest teacher for mistaking his ' good teaching ' for a ' good class.'

Given a quiet period with everyone at work, it is impossible for an outside observer to say whether the quiet is due to internal harmony and interest or to authority and punishment. Both may produce an appearance of good, but only one will be good in reality. Many teachers are unconscious harmonisers of vibrations, a few are consciously so: they both may obtain internal harmony in a class. The 'disciplinarians,' too, quite often secure the appearance of harmony, but it is done by repressing discordant vibrations, 'jamming' them as one might do another's wireless message: some of them even go so far as to 'stop the sound by taking the wires out of the piano.' Even Mme Montessori has this phrase on discipline: "I had to intervene to show with what absolute rigour it is necessary to hinder, and little by little suppress, all those things which we must not do, so that the child may come to discern clearly between good and evil."[1] To use the terms of the later psychologists, one does not suppress since one wishes to avoid repression: it is necessary to 'sublimate.'

(2) Those who desire to confuse appearance and reality are precisely those who wish to model school upon the existing social order, and to prevent change in the present community. The lines of cleavage in the society of school are essential to their project: by these means they can be almost sure that the children will later on 'do their duty in that state of life into which it has pleased God to call them.' To them Authority

[1] *The Montessori Method*, Montessori, ch. v. p. 93.

is the breath of life, and an obedient proletariat the essential base of the pyramid of their ordered society, they themselves being seated securely a the top.[1]

We may defer the analysis of the sanctions upon which Authority relies.[2] Most of us know how they work in School, the list of impositions, fines, extra work, detention, corporal punishment, and the rest. They are accepted by the parents of this generation because they were used upon them as children in the past, and because most parents use them themselves upon their children. The phrase *in loco parentis* means "in a position of special authority." None the less, authority is a transgression of a law of life: it ultimately replaces discord by discord and not by harmony. In essence it is a symptom of the disease of modern coexistence, that same disease which destroyed the communities of old.

When School is a Community.

The class does not remain a community for long: it splits and recombines for individual advantage. There is a constant regrouping of mentalities around one aspect of the subject or another: a practical science class will combine according to its 'apparatus environment': a history class forms constantly new mental communities. For example, in a lesson on the Civil War some side with Cromwell, some with Charles: in one on Industrialism some are for the employers,

[1] Ch. XIV. [2] Ch. XIII.

some with the men who invented new machines, some with the 'hands' who broke them. As the hour strikes, the class breaks up, and joins a 'going-community' to other rooms, there to recombine in fresh communities.

It is at this stage, when all combine for the purpose of change, that school may fairly be called a community, i.e. when it is out of class. Adding the periods of assembly, or morning prayers, or meals, or a school concert, we reach a very small percentage (perhaps 15 per cent.) of the school year to which the theory of school as a community applies. For 85 per cent. it is not one, but many, constantly changing, recombining, breaking down and being built up again.

What School really Is.

We have seen that school is a place to which child-life comes to continue its evolution, that only in a very few cases the life-force of the child is frankly accepted as the central fact of education, that for only a small part of the year is school a single community. What is it, then? It is an organisation which presents an amazing network of customs, conventions, regulations, rules, rewards and punishments. In it social status is a powerful influence, separating servants from children, putting domestic staff in a different compartment to teaching staff, and keeping in special one for the Head. It is clamped together into a solid mass by Authority and Tradition. What madness is this? What connection is there between growth and life and evolution and this mummery of pomp and circumstance? As a survival, an old custom revived perhaps at festivals, with costumes and dances fitting the occasion, it might take its place in chronological order in a pageant of historic scenes. But as a serious attempt to deal with pulsating forces of life striving toward evolution it is a mockery. Were it not plain that it is maintained for the purpose of securing adult obedience to authority and the continuance of the present social order, it would be incredible even as a dream. One thing alone makes it possible as an environment, the child-life which streams through and over it, and will in the end wash it away, as the rain and the rivers sweep away the hills.

SUMMARY OF PART IV

COMMUNITY of effort does not depend upon authority, but on the natural controls evolved by daily life, e.g. common sense, sympathy, tact, self-reliance, creative work, voluntary association, and the like. Those who wield authority do not recognise such controls, but believe that compulsion is the real sanction of law, and in relying upon it have devastated the world.

An individual forms part of many communities during the course of a single day, communities of which all those who partake in his activities are members. A man reading a book is a member of a mental community, either sympathising with the author, subject or style, or with other readers —or in opposition to them.

The 'community of school' is a well-worn phrase which expresses a commonly accepted idea. On analysis however the so-called community is found to be divided by well-marked lines of cleavage, largely social in character, reproducing on a small scale what is mistakenly called the 'community' or state or nation. So far from being a community, school is many communities: only in a small percentage of a year is it one. From the coexistence of the individuals in it spring countless changes of form. The attempt to clamp all together into a rigid unity is the outcome of the purpose of a group to control the later (adult) activities of those who are at present scholars. The final perfection of school will come not from the activities of such a group, but from the lives of the children themselves.

PART V

THE COMMUNITY
(iii) DISEASE

CHAPTER XIII

COMMUNITIES AND STATES

An example of government :	147
Group discord	148
Russia	149
Germany	150
Italy :	150
America (the United States)	152
France	153
Hungary	155
Great Britain	156
The causes and symptoms of disease in States	158

CHAPTER XIV

THE DISEASED COMMUNITY

The constitution of Groups A and B	163
Group A and education	165
The schools of Groups A and B	167
The promise of health	169

CHAPTER XV

THE DISEASES OF AUTHORITY

Community under compulsion impossible	171
The mechanism of compulsion	172
The discords of B	174
The reactions of B to authority	177
Summary of Part V	181

CHAPTER XIII

COMMUNITIES AND STATES

An Example of Government.

A SINGLE day presents to the mind so many instances of coexistence, such an enormous mass of detail and so many symptoms of that life-force which informs us, that it is almost impossible to classify and analyse them owing to sheer superfluity of material. In addition to definitions and a simple formula it is necessary to have clearly before one an example (a standard, test-case, or measure) which may serve as a type with which fresh instances may be compared. It is especially important to secure a clear and vivid concept of government and its functions.

Example. 'Government' and 'governing' as an aid to co-operation in securing individual advantage is a fundamental factor in coexistence. Derived from a Latin word, *gubernare* = to steer, it has changed from its original simple meaning: a similar alteration has taken place with 'prime minister,' which once meant first server, or chief helper.

No better example of government could be found than the Calais boat making Dover harbour, its steersman very literally the governor of that mixed community of travellers drawn from all parts of the Continent, and for an hour or so united by the common purpose of crossing the Channel without the need of swimming. A gentle touch against the quay and his government is over : the passengers stream across the gangways, to meet another example of a later meaning of the word, as customs officials and passport officers interpose their barriers against free individual movement and free interchange of goods.

Group Discord.

When the community no longer serves the advantage of group B, and its members wish to change the existing social order, or even to break away and recombine, group A perhaps refuses its consent. B is then in a state of discord with A : passive resistance becomes more active, until A asserts its authority over B by various means. The latent period ensuing on the first discord merges into mutual opposition, which renders co-existence impossible. Repression of A or B tends, as always, to exaggerate the symptoms of disease ; the common chord of harmony gives place to jarring vibrations of varying disruptive power, and a condition results which shows itself in disturbances, strikes, riots, insurrections, rebellions, or in extreme cases civil war. It is impossible to escape the conclusion that such discords are typical of every so-called State in the world to-day ; not one but has its clear-cut cleavage between A and B. It is usual to ascribe this condition to the general upheaval of 1914, but this is to confuse symptoms with the disease which causes them, to mistake the rash for the fever. The war which began in 1914 'broke out' then like any other rash, but the disease or discord from which it sprang had been latent in the body politic for centuries. War is an intermittent fever the sources of which are in all diseased communities: it is not enough to try to suppress its symptoms: it is necessary to resolve the discords and to recreate internal harmony in the communities of the world. For the present it will be enough to examine the diseases of those organisms which are known as States.

Russia. For long enough it has been obvious that common purpose and advantage had ceased to exist between the governors and the governed in this State. It is unnecessary to give details of the discords which rent it from top to bottom, to repeat the well-known tale of officialdom, of government perverted from its proper function, of authority at bay, of repression and punishment run riot,[1] of peasant degradation and its counterpart of urban vice. Groups A and B were armed to the teeth, and Reds and Whites fought for their group ideals. In vain a more civilised Czar strove to put an end to the struggle, only to fall a victim to B or A.[2] The State, disintegrated by internal disease, fell asunder when its external membrane was pierced by foreign war. And in the natural course of life its parts began to re-

[1] *The House of the Dead*, Dostoieffsky.
[2] *The Vultures*, Seton Merriman.

combine, at first in smaller groups : this was the process known to the outside world as revolution, the new cells or units being called Soviets. As with the Indians of North America (Ch. VIII), their further evolution has been interrupted by other States, whose A groups dread the coming change, whose B groups might have welcomed it.

Germany. The same group-discord racked the State for decades. Enormous industrial development prevented the formation of a very poor B; the economic level of its members was never so low as in Russia. There was however an extremely rich group A, controlling a powerful military system which effectively enslaved group B. The intermediate group (the intelligentsia or professional class) tended to constant dissolution and re-coherence about the nuclei of A or B. The twentieth century saw the main line of cleavage between governors and governed develop into a chasm, though the groups never became real communities with a common purpose. A was financial and military, whilst B was a vague and incoherent mass of occupational interests. The State as a whole exhibited the usual tendency to division and recombination which is natural to all coexistence; it also showed a particularly well marked condition of repressive activity on the part of A.[1]

Italy. This State differs from other Western European ' nations ' in being a more recent for-

---

[1] See *Jena oder Sedan ?* Bayerlein, for the military side of group A. A striking picture of the financial A in relation to B is to be found in *Die Ehre*, Sudermann.

mation. The confusion of community with State which obscures the minds of observers in England is less possible here : its long history of separation, its republican tradition, its comparatively recent regrouping around the nucleus of Rome, have permitted the survival of the outer membranes of its constituent groups. There is the usual financial-governing class, the urban-industrial, and a well defined rural-agricultural population. The financial-governing group is the Italian A : for some time past it has contrived to separate the other two, and to profit by the jealousies it has been able to foment between them. B (urban) and C (rural) might have been driven further apart in the common post-war economic ruin, but the repression exercised by A has brought them together. Here as in other modern States we find a group which dreads change opposed to others which must have change or sink into slavery.

The efforts of the urban group B to adapt their community to their needs was observable in their occupation of the great factories in 1920. The rural C exhibited the same tendency in 1920–1921 in their occupation of large estates and their attempts to subdivide them among members of their group. Both B and C however were repressed by A through the activities of what was virtually a 'white army,' the body of young men known as the Fascisti. These were an informal and unofficial volunteer community of ex-soldiers of A sympathies, who raided the country-side and the towns with the avowed purpose of destroying the central nervous system of B and C. Their brutalities and foolish excesses and the reprisals which these aroused [1] are indications of a deep-seated malignant disease in the state, infecting each group and lowering the vitality of all: they exhibit in a marked form the symptoms of the old struggle between Guelphs and Ghibellines, with the further consequences of post-war complications. Not even an untrained observer could well confuse community and state in Italy.

America, U.S. Enormous area, mingled races, and division into urban and rural—and governing and governed—groups, conceal to some extent the diseases of this State. Yet though the symptoms are confused, we may see groups A and B in opposition in the activities of the Secret Police, in the conduct of the financial-governing group A from 1914 onward, the fierce repression practised against group B in its attempts to secure common advantage from its coexistence with A. Here one may observe the same cessation of community, the same latent period, culminating in repression by A and retaliation by B. There is however a still more striking line of cleavage, the colour-line, which of itself would render it impossible to classify the United States as a community. As States they may be united: as a community they have not yet been conceived.

Where Italy or France or Germany or England or even Spain has been enabled by geographical conditions to confine its 'native' wars to 'native' territory, the United States are faced with a

[1] See "The Story of the Fascisti," *Nation* and *Athenæum*, May 14, 1921.

running sore actually within their borders. It is an inherited disease which they contracted from their parents [1]: they were attacked by it before they commenced their separate existence, and to this day they bear the marks of it for all the world to see. The same infection has ravaged South Africa from its earliest infancy. It is perhaps the most striking example the world can offer of the consequences which follow disregard of a fundamental principle of life. Without voluntary association community is impossible, and without community evolution ceases.

France. It is unnecessary to analyse this State in detail. It presents much the same urban and rural division as Italy, and is as markedly characterised by cleavage into governors and governed as other 'nations.' To some extent the fusion between the various communities which marked the earlier stages of the war remains. This fusion was remarkable for its temporary completeness, the vast majority of the inhabitants vibrating with a passionate energy in the defence of what they had come to regard as a community, and the

[1] *Principal Navigations*, Hakluyt: "Master John Hawkins . . . he being amongst other particulars assured that Negroes were very good marchandise in Hispaniola, and that store of Negroes might easily bee had upon the coast of Guinea, he resolved with himselfe to make triall thereof, and communicated that devise with his worshipfull friendes of London: namely with Sir Lionell Ducket, Sir Thomas Lodge, M. Gunston his father-in-law, Sir William Winter, M. Bromfield and others, all which persons liked so well of his intention, that they became liberall contributers and adventurers in the action. . . . He passed to Sierra Leone . . . where he . . . got into his possession, partly by the sword and partly by other means, to the number of three hundred negroes." (Sir John Hawkins' First Voyage to the W. Indies, 1562, 1563.)

continuance of which they therefore considered necessary for their evolution. Yet their past history shows that neither under Louis XIV nor Napoleon nor during the Revolution was there any community which could be called France. The boundaries of the state included even under *le roi soleil* (the king who was the sun, i.e. Louis XIV) both poor and rich, split asunder by an economic chasm: the Revolution showed an internecine struggle between groups A and B unrivalled in ferocity. The dominion of group A was surely obvious in the railway strike which M. Briand crushed. Since the Great Peace the State of France presents a combination of the symptoms exhibited by Germany and Italy: she is still in process of division, and with her—as elsewhere—the financial-governing group A is first to recombine, if indeed it ever dissolved. There is however a symptom in France which is unusual among white communities: the colour cleavage tends to become blurred, and racial antagonism to lose its force. Owing to national exhaustion group A is unable to rely upon the modern means of repressing B, i.e. conscription,[1] yet it has set itself the task of controlling B not only in France but in Germany as well,—an experiment in internationalism of a doubtful kind. Thus, whilst the United States countenances what is virtually a civil war upon its negro members, group A in France welcomes its negro troops as equal citizens, equal at least in liability to military service. These troops render valuable aid in repressing the German group B.

[1] Compare Ch. X, "Voluntary Association," p. 120.

Quite apart from the echoes of discord which such a policy must ultimately produce in Africa, its immediate result upon the population of Germany has proved appalling in the extreme: whole districts have been inoculated with a virus of hatred and loathing in itself powerful enough to produce another war.[1] A horror of this magnitude may well provide a stimulus sharp enough to cause group B in France and Germany to unite in opposition to the cynicism of their rulers, and thus form a real community.

Hungary. The upheaval caused by the war of 1914 and the almost complete destruction of the older forms of government in this part of Europe, coupled with the breakdown of communications and the cessation of supplies of imported wheat, have caused a recombination of individuals into an agricultural community of simple form.[2] This is in marked contrast to the almost universal collapse of industrial communities, and serves to indicate the form which human coexistence might be expected to take under the more natural conditions of earth-work rather than factory-work, e.g. in Lincolnshire rather than in Lancashire. The need of food has placed power in the hands of those who can produce it, and by a turn of fortune group B is able to dictate to group A. The change has not been made without reprisals on the part of B for its long-endured repression,

---

[1] Compare *Schwarze am Rhein: ein Weltproblem* (Black Troops on the Rhine: a World Problem), Eberlein.

[2] See articles in *Nation* and *Athenæum*, June 11, etc., 1921, by Thompson and Fodor, " The Green Rising."

yet it is valuable in its results, as showing the broad lines of man's present stage of evolution. He appears as essentially independent, narrow or even vindictive in character, a believer in freedom for his own activities and a convinced supporter of private property, ready to co-operate for further advantage, and unattracted by schemes of dominion, a type common to any system of small holdings, observable in a much more evolved stage in Denmark.

Great Britain. Every inhabitant of these islands has at one time or another been made aware of the theory that he is a member of a community, that the community is coextensive with the population and the islands, and that the sacrifice of the individual to the community is desirable and on occasion necessary. This trinity of inaccuracy is the very foundation of the religion of the state. On examination what do we find?

The most cursory glance shows three very definite subdivisions in this island alone, three parts clamped together by authority for what are said to be common purpose. A fourth part, geographically isolated from the three, maintains to-day a struggle for separation which has lasted some seven hundred years. Confining our attention to this island, we find that it presents an urban-rural cleavage, that both urban and rural districts are cross-divided by the modern financial-governing line. Here, as in other States, we have groups A and B: practically every centre of industry provides examples of extreme wealth and of a poverty rivalling even that of Russia.

We find individuals dying of hunger, for we have always a number for whom there is no chance of work. We see a growth of the military-financial group which once was as typical of Germany as it now is of France. If group B be taken to include the workers, we find group B itself a conglomerate mass of opposing interests, tending to cohere round the nuclei of their trade organisations : we find these organisations split again into A and B, imitating in their ignorance the very errors which have separated them and their employers.

These insulated groups are held together by the sanctions of authority; where necessary their attempts at separation and recombination are overawed by that same White Army which we have seen in Russia, Italy and other States : the recent formation of a Defence Force is neither more nor less than group A's effort to constrain group B, not for AB advantage but to maintain a form of coexistence in which B loses whilst A gains. The theory that this State is a community will not hold water for a moment. The inhabitants of the island, like all other human beings, exhibit community and voluntary association in countless variety from day to day, but to suppose them all combined in one great coexistence is demonstrably false. Indeed, to the common sense of the individual no proof is needed : his heaped-up experience of the past tells him at once that Community and State are not the same.

The Causes and Symptoms of Disease in States.

Comparing our observations and assembling the factors common to each State-problem, we find in all modern States a condition of disease. In each we see a varying but well-marked cohesion round a financial-military-governing group (the military aspect being less fundamental than the financial). We have in every specimen of State a group A which controls the government of the whole primarily for A and not AB advantage. The principle of free association and the natural controls of coexistence (Ch. X) are set at naught, and compulsion in every form is substituted in their place. So far from there being community of purpose in a State between A and B, the A community finds its mutual aid in the A community of other States. So we may trace an international group A with activities in every State: being in control of government and therefore of trade and transport and communications, it is more evolved, more sensitive to stimulus and quicker in reaction than the loosely organised yet equally international B groups. Insofar as A depends for existence on repression of B, A is diseased: to the extent that A uses other A help to repress its own group B the disease of A and B is international.

We are thus compelled to admit that what we observe in modern States is a stage of evolution in which communities present the symptoms of chronic endemic disease, produced by a self-generated poison which is the product of the disregard of an essential principle of coexistence. Within the borders of a single State the symptoms of this poisoning are known as riots, insurrections, rebellions or even civil war. When from time to time two States or groups of States are involved, the common sickness flares up in the deadly epidemic of war.

CHAPTER XIV

THE DISEASED COMMUNITY

THE repression of B by A invariably produces a condition of disease, in a community or between individuals. It is worth while to examine in further detail the condition of the State in which we live.

In no small degree as a result of dislocation of population and its congestion in industrial centres, the free association of individuals in communities has been for long impeded. A simple example will suffice to show the process. A man and his wife settle down near the mill or factory in which one or both are working. They have children, who are subjected to the processes of State education, processes not necessarily fitting them for free association as adults. After a time these children themselves go out to earn a living : there is neither time nor opportunity for them to look round for creative work suited to their personal need of evolution : they consider themselves fortunate to get work at the same place as their parents—or as near home as possible. So far from being able to attain a higher phase of evolution, they are thrown back upon the necessity of supplying their elemental needs. They are not superior to their environment at all : they are as much slaves of environment as are wolves or ants or bees. Growing dissatisfaction with such an existence, multiplied ten-thousandfold and more, produces a relaxation of the bonds of community, and especially of mental community. Individuals forced by economic necessity to remain members of a community which compels them to live in a poor street in a town are likely to attempt to change a social order which secures them little advantage. In this they are perfectly justified, for community without common advantage does not exist,—and if it did it would be mere slavery. Much the same factors influence the agricultural labourer. Thus, in an island where the majority of the people are so poor as to have little or no margin of financial security, few of the many communities are able to hold out sufficient inducements to their members to secure continuance. We have then on the one hand a marked tendency to division of community, and separation with the avowed purpose of recombination. This natural process should be assisted in every way.

On the other hand we have shareholders, managers, directors and financial magnates confronted with the possibility of strikes, of inferior or irregular production, of disturbances in industry which cannot but prove harassing to them, and may result in serious loss. There is of course no reason why a financial magnate should not lose his fortune and be compelled by poverty to earn his living in what were once his own works : it is however not to be expected that he will do so with any readiness or enthusiasm. This is precisely the problem which presented itself so strikingly in Italy in 1920. The situation is further complicated by the fact that, having earnestly implored your workpeople to offer their lives in defence of what they have been taught to regard as their community (viz. the State), you are in no position to oppose their demand—when they return—for a fairer share of the common advantage.

Here there enters another factor which complicates affairs still more. The false doctrine that the State is the community is held by none more strongly than by the well-to-do: they have been expressly taught it in their schools as the true political (even religious) creed. Interest and belief thus combine to stiffen their attitude towards group B. And, as government is in their hands, and law on their side, they have no hesitation in teaching group B their place in the ordained scheme of things. They do not shrink from threatening force openly. For proof, it is only necessary to read again the speeches of the chief representative of 'popular' government at the time of the lockout in the coal trade in 1921. These and the measures subsequently taken are convincing evidence of the cessation of community.

It would however be a slipshod and ignorant observer who contented himself with the division of the State into governors and governed, two clear-cut groups in violent opposition. (This is a fault common to many would-be reformers.) The opposition is violent, it is true, but groups A and B are by no means sharply defined. The third

THE DISEASED COMMUNITY

group, observable in every modern State (the intelligentsia or professional), being less stable, tends to dissolve and recombine around an A or B nucleus. This of course is natural. What is more difficult to allow for is the filtration from A to B or B to A. Let us consider the latter first.

THE CONSTITUTION OF GROUPS A AND B.

Group B is mostly composed of workers: it is also divided and subdivided in all directions into occupational communities, of miners, railwaymen, transport workers of all kinds, small traders, ' one man businesses,' etc. It has a well marked line of sex cleavage, due to the under-payment of women as compared with men. What binds all together into a physical community of poverty is the urgent elemental need of food and shelter. But since each community seems to secure less than a living margin to its members, each community tends to dissolve and recombine. And all the time those who see an opportunity of ' improving their position ' do so, so that even the poorest community has its group A and group B. These groups A tend to cohere about the financial-governing group: the groups B are driven to cohere about a larger ' working class ' B nucleus. Hence the central A group is no simple collection of ' rich ' or ' well-to-do ' or ' capitalists ' or ' parasites,' but a financial-governing group of rich, etc., with ramifications extending even to the slums of a factory or seaport town, or the poorest cottage in a country village.

Again, since he has evolved beyond the animals

by reason of his mentality, man tends to form mental as well as physical communities (see Ch. XI). In proportion to his evolution man combines in mental communities: this directly affects the members of group A in every small occupational community. Consider for example the position of a railway guard who is nearing the end of his service. He has saved some money and invested it in War Loan or some good stock: he has a tidy house, a wife and children. He looks forward to retirement and simple ease and comfort: his children have the best education he can afford, and promise well. He reads his daily paper, and thinks he knows. He is a group A man: not for him the perils of change, the vapourings of the Socialist or Communist. He has no knowledge of evolution, of the history of community among animals or man: he feels himself free and independent. So he coheres about the nucleus A, and gives his support to the existing social order, literally incapable of conceiving that it is in a condition of disease, shocked when his children see through his error, find themselves unable to earn as much as they need, and grow sour in consequence, or even worse. He is all for the Defence Force, and never dreams it may be really used—at least not in his suburb.

Thus group A has no clear outline: it is surrounded by the hangers-on of privilege. These may include archbishops, educationists, sergeants, works-managers, foremen, shop-walkers, magistrates, business men, generals, retired colonels, government officials, town councillors, the public hangman, university students, clerks, trade union officials, clergy, ministers (cabinet, prime or denominational), experts of all kinds, sociologists, publicans, journalists, professors or policemen,—all these and more, with their wives and families and dependents. Group A includes those who have, and think they might lose by change: group B comprises those to whom change is the only escape from virtual slavery.

Group A and Education.

The obvious need of change in the social order is forcing mankind to study the conditions of coexistence, and both groups issue textbooks of A or B character. Group A has the advantage, since the control of education is virtually in its hands, and some of the works issued on its behalf are well worth examination. One in particular is of interest: it may almost be considered the official handbook on the subject.[1] The standing of its author, as well as the contents of the work in question, mark it as typically A. It is perhaps natural that he should choose England and France, "the French, but still more the British and the American nations," as the highest forms of human community yet reached in the history of the world: this is a matter of opinion, and as such is not to be criticised,—though the members of group B may consider his ideas unconvincing in the light of their daily environment. When however

[1] *The Group Mind*, McDougall, ch. xiii ("Nations of the Higher Type").

he states[1] that in an army "the private soldier in the ranks remains a free agent performing truly volitional actions" one may reasonably doubt his facts.

We have seen that communities are not limited by frontiers, that A and B are international in their activities, whether they are governing groups, armament firms, shipping companies, trade unions, Red Cross organisations, combinations of individuals against famine or disease, religious orders, and so on. Even supposing for a moment that an army is the means by which the State may be defended, we know that State is not Community, but a complex of communities in a condition of disease. We do not forget recent examples of the imminent use of the Army in this country, nor its activities in Ireland and elsewhere during the past: we are under no delusions as to its connection with group A. But, taking his statement for what it is worth, let us examine it in the light of the evolution of coexistence. An army is pre-eminently an instrument for the repression of vibrations: it is almost entirely of one sex,—indeed, in its most active moments it is supposed to be entirely so, since women are not yet permitted in the trenches. It is the very opposite of voluntary association: we gave up that illusion years ago. It is the negation of the principle of free combination, since very few may contract out of it at will. It is the antithesis of that power of creative work which characterises human nature, for its 'common end' is destruction. And as for common advan-

[1] Ch. iii, "The Highly Organised Group."

tage between its members, neither in pay nor privilege nor in possibilities of supplying elemental needs is there community between officer and private: no private would dare to sit down to supper at the general's table, though even fishermen and carpenters might eat and drink with Christ. Even in a diseased community it is impossible to conceive an example of human activity more diametrically opposed to the purpose of coexistence than this. There can be few more amazing instances of un-reason even in the textbooks of group A: in its failure to grasp the meaning of human life it almost equals the following example from a work by an expert on disorders of the mind. Amongst the examples of nervous diseases classified by Southard,[1] and indexed under the heading 'Sympathy with the enemy,' is one of a German officer who refused to let his men fire upon the enemy, "because the idea came forcibly to him that the enemy soldiers had wives and children." A community in which instinctive common sense such as this is diagnosed as neurasthenia is indeed diseased.

The Schools of Groups A and B.

The ideal which inspires the schools of group A may be summed up in the phrase 'loyalty to a tradition.' They provide one of the most striking examples of the herd-instinct the world has ever seen. Nowhere will there be found a readier response to the call of danger to the group, whether

[1] *Shell Shock and Neuro-Psychiatry*, Southard, p. 851.

the smaller group of school or that larger one the State,—which has for so long been their playground. No sacrifice can be too great to ask, none that will not be instantly and cheerfully made for this ancient foundation of government whose stones must ever be cemented anew with the life-blood of the individual. Their discipline is based on punishment, corporal or other: so, when their scholars take their place as servants of the State they believe in force as the ultimate control of coexistence; they carry on the Imperial tradition in the spirit of Alexander, Jenghiz Khan or Napoleon,[1] thus hindering human evolution. Freedom within the group is their prerogative, and authority over others their inheritance.

Since the control of State education is in the hands of A, the schools of group B are infected with the same traditions of repression: but where the group A child is being taught to govern, the offspring of group B learns to be governed, and grows up accepting and handing on the belief in external authority as the ultimate security for the existing social order: they also learn that the State is their community. Owing to the enormous size of the classes in State schools, each hour becomes a daily practice in repression; the children thus grow up with the conviction that there are two types of human being, the governed and the governors.[2]

[1] Government Report on the Rising in the Punjab.

[2] Cf. the remarks of the magistrate of the West London Police Court (December 1921) to a County Council schoolboy, who brought an action against his teacher for beating him for drawing on his slate during lessons.

The Promise of Health.

There are in almost every school a few teachers who coexist with their classes on a basis of cooperative mentality: there is in every class a majority who will so respond to such treatment as to make it always worth while,—the rest may be trusted to follow their example. In childhood and in adult life there is that innate belief in freedom which is the result of past experience of evolution: there is the common sense on which mankind instinctively relies: there are the natural controls of coexistence to which men turn ever more and more: there are communities which in spite of government restrictions continually overflow or filter through the boundaries of States. Finally there is that life-force—common to all humanity—which has driven and is driving mankind along the road of evolution. In this, and in these, lies the promise of health: without them we might as well resign ourselves to disease and sink beneath the scum of its corruption and decay.

CHAPTER XV

THE DISEASES OF AUTHORITY

WHERE A and B coexist, their relationship is the product of certain definite and observable factors: these factors will be (1) individual, (2) communal. Each individual is (*a*) a receiver of vibrations, (*b*) a harmoniser of vibrations, (*c*) a generator of vibrations; these cover his connection with the external world: internally, each responds to the vibrations of that life-force which is all pervading. Stating this in terms of religion one may say that when two human beings coexist their conduct is conditioned by their nature, by their environment, and by their harmony with God. A possible source of confusion arises here, since it is customary to regard God as a final court of appeal, and careless reasoning is apt to be content with the assumption that authority is of God. It is essential to be clear on this point: the authority of God, or—if you will—the law of life, is but the control of the human being by an eternal force to which the eternal in him (his soul) responds. The authority of man, in this State, resides ultimately in the Lord Chancellor and the Commander-in-Chief, the latter subject ultimately to the Prime Minister— as the head of the civil power. It is inexcusable to continue to confuse any of these no doubt perfectly respectable citizens with the Supreme Being. The soul of man knows well enough what he shall render to Cæsar and what to God.

COMMUNITY UNDER COMPULSION IMPOSSIBLE.

When A and B combine for common advantage, they make agreements which shall regulate their activities: when they cease their common action and one (or both) desires to withdraw from the community, community has ceased to live: it is dead.[1] It follows that the agreements which had as their object the regulation of their activities together also cease to be binding. It is common sense (and strangely enough also common law) that agreements made under duress (e.g. obtained by force or threats) cannot be held to be binding. It is of the essence of a contract for common purposes that it should be entered into voluntarily.[2] (It is unfair that the rules of a school should be held to bind a child unless and until the child understands and accepts them: it is monstrous that the regulations of an industrial school or a prison should be held binding upon those sent there by force.) These are the fundamental principles of the doctrine of 'government by consent of the governed' of which we once were so justly proud. They are also directly in accord with the facts of life, and for this reason are the very mainspring of coexistence: their disregard produces

[1] Cessation of common purpose and its consequences are considered more fully in Ch. IX, p. 109).
[2] Compare "The Natural Controls of Coexistence," p. 120.

disease, with all the inevitability of ancient fate. What else should transgression of the laws of life produce but disease and death?

The Mechanism of Compulsion.

When B, unable to obtain the consent of A, attempts to withdraw from the AB community, A first of all points out that it is "against the law," the law being the agreements entered into by both, and now terminated as the community is terminated. Should B persist, A proceeds to compel him by punishment: he 'asserts his authority' over B, i.e. his claim to impose his will on B: the ultimate sanction of A's authority over B is force. Let us state this in terms of vibrations. In order that A and B may co-operate, the individual internal harmonies of A and B have been tuned to a sympathetic rhythm in which both together produce an AB chord. This chord becomes the internal harmony of their community. B, desiring further evolution, finds that the community from which he hoped so much is actively hindering him: after due notice and with—to him—sufficient reason given, he ceases rhythmic vibration with A, and proceeds to tune himself to other harmonies or rhythms. A, finding protests useless, begins to emit vibrations which shall either (1) thrust their rhythm upon B and once more establish their common chord, or (2) so interrupt B's vibrations as to make it impossible for him to vibrate alone or to tune himself to another series, or (3) so beat upon his nervous system as to incapacitate it

(i) temporarily, (ii) permanently, for further vibration, harmonious or otherwise. This is the mechanism of compulsion stated generally in terms of vibration : it will be found applicable to particular cases of every kind. It applies to a teacher coercing a pupil, to members of a trade union opposing the employment of non-union men, to magistrate and prisoner, husband and wife, or to a larger or stronger State menacing a smaller or weaker, etc.[1]

The result produced in B is discord, and the destruction of internal harmony either temporarily or permanently : it may cause unhappiness, sickness, or in extreme cases insanity or death. Frequently the external appearance of co-operation may be obtained ; at times the co-operation may be real, should B be as it were hypnotised by the treatment. This however does not justify its use ; the central objection to compulsion is not that it *may* (or may not) cause damage or disease, but that by substituting the will of A for that of B it *must* weaken or destroy the will of B. It is beside the point to say " B does not mind," or " B is the better for it," or " What else could one do ? " or to choose some apparently frivolous example in which the damage to B is minute at the time. One has to remember that by employing compulsion one accustoms B to use compulsion as his control in coexistence, and B may not always remain a prisoner for theft, but come out and commit robbery with violence. One has to consider that B as a child accustomed to com-

[1] For summary of these mechanisms, see chart at end of chapter.

pulsion may when grown up be in command at Amritsar or elsewhere, or in charge of a factory, or become a member of a government negotiating with a State which demands self-determination.

Neither is it an argument that B (1) does not feel the effect of compulsion, or (2) likes it, or (3) sees the justice of it. In (1) the conduct of A is not affected by the blunted state of B : in (2) it does not excuse A because B is a slave or a pervert : in (3) it does not free A from responsibility to say that B is ignorant of a law of life, or in a state of mental confusion or misinformed repentance. Whatever the state of B, when A asserts his will over him at the expense of B's will he contravenes a law of life and, either in himself or in B or both, produces a state of disease.

The Discords of B.

The reactions of B to compulsion take many and various forms, ranging from a dull distaste or boredom to the most panic convulsions of terror : any or all groups of nerve cells may be stimulated or deadened, and there are countless possibilities of variation in their condition and their combination. As with other human activities, we may recognise three main classes of emotion, bodily, mental and spiritual. It would be useless to attempt a full description of each : the bibliography of the subject alone would itself fill a volume, and the technical words and phrases used in the study of mind—whether normal or diseased —are unintelligible to a lay student : also, opinion

THE DISEASES OF AUTHORITY 175

differs so enormously as to cause or effect or symptom or cure that even prolonged study may not do more than increase our uncertainty. It is however possible to suggest a general statement of—let us say—fear, its mechanism and its results, which may serve as a guide in studying the disease which is produced alike in individuals and in communities by the negation of freedom. 'Fear' is a vague name for a condition known to everyone: it is preferable to replace it by something more precise and at the same time more general, and less steeped in associations which may mislead us. Let us then consider the condition of B when 'about-to-be-compelled' by A,—e.g. a child awaiting reproof, a prisoner hearing sentence, a convict about to be thrashed or hanged, a nation about to be invaded, even an animal about to be killed.

At the outset we must distrust external appearance as a guide, just as we should consider analysis of the bodily tissues after execution to be useless as an indication of the last living mental states of the prisoner. The reactions of B depend on his individual nature: no set rules can be laid down. We shall best approach the problem by recalling the vibrations of A when about to compel, or actually compelling: these aim at the reconstitution, interruption, or incapacitation of the vibrations of B. Between the very slightest and the most extreme disturbances of B there extends the whole range of human tragedy and horror, from mere surprise to the complete extinction of life or reason. As in the darkness of the sky there move not only the known stars but also countless dark bodies which have never chanced to come to light, so the history of compulsion holds not merely the known records of sieges, tortures, executions, buryings alive, sentences, cruelties deliberate or unintentional, but also those untold repressions, agonies of mind, sufferings in silence, madnesses, which go to swell the frightful sum of human misery.

The normal condition of B as a receiver, harmoniser and generator of vibrations is the product of his nature, his environment, and his internal harmony. The compulsion of A is a change in his environment to which he will respond: his response then depends upon (1) his nature, (2) his internal harmony. To take (2) first: should it be perfect, the acts of A will leave him undisturbed; history presents numerous cases of martyrs whose conviction, philosophy or religion have led them smiling to the rack, the block, the stake, the crucifix, the fire. These need no help, though some achieve harmony only by superhuman exertions: indeed it is common for them to realise the greater needs of A. Our problem narrows to the reactions of a B whose elemental nature is less evolved, lacking internal harmony. We have already seen (Ch. III) that the resolution of discord is essential to human progress, that it may occupy not only childhood but the whole period of adult life,—also, that success depends upon the individual will.

THE DISEASES OF AUTHORITY 177

THE REACTIONS OF B TO AUTHORITY.

In normal health the nervous system of B is sending constant unconscious messages to veins, arteries and every organ of his body to ensure its proper function and its general nourishment: his mind, conscious or subconscious, is always working: his body is in a state of activity. The resultant of these life-vibrations is that fluctuating quantity which we call personality. Let us suppose him a child playing, and that his activities have disturbed an adult, who asserts authority with a harsh word, a gesture, a blow, or any stimulus sufficient to cause this particular B a shock.

The first effect is an interference with all existing nervous activity: nourishment, mental state, movement, personality change at once: the normal balance of nervous impulse is disturbed. The second effect is a damming-up or repression of nervous impulse. The third is its discharge—exaggerated in consequence of the repression—along paths which instinct or habit or chance association may determine. These processes may be observed almost anywhere by anyone.

Observe that this is a single sequence, a unit of reaction; also that there may be an antecedent and a consequent period. We may now consider a case which exhibits (1) Antecedent period, (2) Reaction unit, (3) Consequent period. Let us suppose a child about to undergo corporal punishment: there will have been a previous assertion of authority. *Antecedent period.* The period of waiting will be marked by fluctuation of personality and destruction of internal harmony. *Reaction*. The effects of this will be intensified, particularly the first (interference) : the second (damming-up) will be continued over into the third (discharge), with exaggeration, especially in connection with the first. *Consequent period.* The chief effect will be mental: it may produce the appearance of the desired result,—it certainly will produce a number of other consequences which it is impossible to estimate accurately.

In both these cases the crude stimulus of compulsion was physical: it may equally well be mental, e.g. with a child suspected of theft. *Antecedent*, a period of suspicion and being under a cloud: *Reaction unit*, rebuke before the assembled school accompanied by pardon : *Consequent*, the rest of the term. Such a combination of influences may well demoralise internal harmony for a lifetime.

It is not necessary to use even a loud tone of voice in the assertion of authority: consider the following example. *Antecedent*, imprisonment, trial for murder, and conviction : *Reaction unit*, sentence, in a quiet measured tone, passionless, inhuman, " to be hanged by the neck until you are dead, and may the Lord have mercy on your soul ": *Consequent*, a period of waiting. Observe as it were in yourself the reaction unit, (1) an interference with all existing nervous activity, (2) a damming-up of nervous energy, (3) its discharge along paths which instinct or habit or chance association may determine. Observe, too, how this attempt to give definite names to human agony lessens your power of sympathy, makes it seem less dreadful, impersonal, almost interesting. Only by a determined effort towards internal harmony, and aided by the common sense which we have all evolved, can we see this particular exercise of Authority as it really is, an agent of repression and destruction, unskilled, incredibly stupid, ghastly, horrible.

As the weapon of a group it is a thousand times more loathsome. Small wonder that its victims sometimes pray for those who use it and know not what they do.

THE COMMUNITY : DISEASE

A'S VIBRATIONS OF COMPULSION.

Individuals or Groups.	Aim. Re-establishment of original Rhythm.	Aim. Interruption of B's new Rhythm.	Aim. Incapacitation of B.	
			Temporary.	Permanent.
A. Teacher, or Parent. B. Child.	command, persuasion, threats, rebuke before others, etc.	making him sit alone, stand in corner, fold arms, etc., punishment.	sending B out of room.	expulsion from school.
A. Trade unionists. B. Non-union men.	argument, threats, picketing.	going on strike.	obstruction or assault.	serious assault or homicide.
A. Magistrate. B. Accused.	advice or caution and discharge.	fine or imprisonment.	imprisonment.	—
A. Judge. B. Accused.	advice or caution and discharge.	fine or imprisonment.	imprisonment.	either life or death sentence.
A. Husband B. Wife	argument, threats.	threats, pursuit, exposure, or assault.	private : assault. public : divorce.	private : murder.

SUMMARY OF PART V

GOVERNMENT as it should be is best exemplified by the steersman bringing the Calais boat into Dover Harbour, where government as it is is represented by passports, customs and other hindrances. Group discord is produced when one group represses the activities of another or denies it freedom. An analysis of Russia, Germany, Italy, America (United States), France, Hungary and Great Britain shows that modern States exhibit the diseases of discord, that group A in each represses group B, and that the communities of these States are diseased. Also, State and community are not the same.

The modern diseased communities cohere round two main nuclei, (1) financial-military-governing, (2) working class, with an unstable and fluctuating (3), the intelligentsia or professional class. There is no clear-cut line between these, and many in (2) might belong to (1) but for their mental community. The education of group A produces a group tradition of governing, that of B a tradition of being governed. Such theories as that the State is a community, or that an army is a community, are false, and produce group discord. The discipline maintained in group schools reacts unfavourably upon international policy, for it depends not on co-operation but on authority.

Authority is an unnatural control, producing

discord and disease, and destroying community—which cannot exist under compulsion. The mechanism of compulsion is calculated for the purpose of producing shock. When A compels B, B exhibits a series of discords capable of definition and description. The reactions of B to authority may also be described simply and clearly, and observed almost daily and almost everywhere. To destroy the internal harmony of an individual or group in order to subject it to authority is unnatural and disastrous.

PART VI

THE FUTURE OF MAN

CHAPTER XVI

THE TENDENCY OF THE INDIVIDUAL

The conditions of evolution	186
Human activities	187
A method of study	188
Individual evolution : aids and hindrances	190
Summary of aids and hindrances	198

CHAPTER XVII

THE TENDENCY OF THE COMMUNITY

Some post-war aids and hindrances	202
A specimen of community	206
General conditions affecting community	208
Two further examples of community	210
Community : Summary	212

CHAPTER XVIII

PLUS OR MINUS ? 216

CHAPTER XVI

THE TENDENCY OF THE INDIVIDUAL

IN the minds of very many there is a vague idea that evolution has something to do with monkeys, and happened about the time of the Flood. They look at cases in museums and say " Isn't it wonderful to think we used to be like that ? " and only very few think " Isn't it ridiculous that we should be like this ? " They have a general impression of man as a wise biped who has learnt to fly, and built a skyscraper, and to-morrow or next year will stand on the roof and start for perfection in an aeroplane. They cannot believe that he has not learnt to fly,—that if he had he would need a new waistcoat because his breastbone would project so far in front and his chest muscles be so huge. They mistake appearance for reality: their hard-bitten materialism remains supremely content with externals: they become increasingly averse from the effort of reasoning. The rich seem drugged with power, the poor with hopelessness.

Yet evolution was, and is, and will be. It *is being* now. To begin to understand it, we have to remember that the past has only just gone, the future is just coming, and that the present is only the moment in which we turn our eyes to look from one to the other. 'Evolution' may be roughly translated "a turning out": how are we going to turn out?

The Conditions of Evolution.

If we consider the evolution of a wheelbarrow, we make certain assumptions: we take it for granted that it has one wheel and two handles, and is intended for use on land, not in the water or the air. A good large wheelbarrow might do for a boat for the children at the seaside: or a Chinaman might put a mast and a sail on it (on land): but whatever happens to it its evolution will be conditioned by its wheelbarrowness, and our discussion of its future will depend upon our clear understanding of what it is. Though we also have to consider what it was, we must start from what it is at present. In the same way, when you ask a friend "What are the conditions of human evolution?" and the friend has no clear idea of what a human being is, you explain that in your opinion man is an organism capable of receiving, harmonising and generating vibrations, and that he has a soul, i.e. that he is partly temporary and partly eternal. If this is correct, and you both agree to accept it, you are in a position to discuss the future of man with the help of your imagination and your common sense. Man's future is not only a hundred or a thousand years hence: if you are discussing it at lunch at a quarter past one, it is essential to remember that

THE TENDENCY OF THE INDIVIDUAL 187

twenty past one is in the future, and that what you decide will influence your own life as well as your friend's, during the afternoon, and to-morrow, and next week.

The evolution of man may then be considered as a 'turning out' of his powers of (1) receiving, (2) harmonising, (3) generating vibrations, and of his soul. Let us see whither the argument takes us: there is none of more fascinating interest. We may not reach the end, or get very far, but we shall at least forget that dull drugged discontent and disappointment which so often blights us: we shall no longer ask "What is the use of anything?" because we shall find some use in everything.

The Study of Human Activities.

Life presents an overwhelming mass of facts to us from day to day, and we cannot all be experts at everything: but we all have our common sense to guide us, and frequently we come across a fact which strikes us as absurd or intolerable,—as for instance that our canals are not used enough, or that large tracts of land are kept for grazing, or that people are herded into towns while the country is being emptied. If we are students of life, we must make our study methodical: the scientist has his 'scientific method of enquiry'; we must make a human method of enquiry.

Take for example our heaped-up towns; we think them vile, our common sense tells us they are unhealthy. Are we to keep them and improve them, or scrap them and make something else? Many remedies suggest themselves, and some seem better than others: which are we to take? Only those which are in line with evolution will give a permanent improvement: which are they? It is here that we need a method of study, a quick rough means of classifying human activities as plus or minus in result. Thus we shall have two aids to the study of life: (1) the common sense which first arrests our attention, (2) a method of finding out if a certain change will give good or bad results.

A Method of Study.

We cannot keep the usual scientific divisions of life into watertight compartments, such as Geology or Anatomy or Hygiene or Sociology: at the risk of being called unscientific we must pool all these and re-divide them. What we need is not so much an index to one book as a catalogue of the whole library. It is good practice to proceed as follows.

1. Divide life-activities into Individual and Communal.
2. Decide whether the fact we are studying has to do with (*a*) Receiving, (*b*) Harmonising, (*c*) Generating vibrations.

    Note.—In considering (*a*), for example the sense of sight, we shall make things simpler by grouping together as sight-organs not merely the eyes but everything which has been invented to help eyes, even though some may in the end harm the eyes: e.g. microscopes. Again, in considering the sense of

THE TENDENCY OF THE INDIVIDUAL 189

touch, we may include under this head everything which helps to improve touch. All these may be grouped under Reception.

3. Distinguish between an activity which merely brings man up to the normal, and one which improves him beyond it. Our industrial civilisation does not always improve man: we may call what merely brings him up to the normal 'Subnormal evolution,' and call the activities which carry him on past the normal to something better 'Supranormal.'

4. Having decided that a remedy or change or an existing activity is one which helps evolution we may call it Plus: if we think it hinders evolution we may call it Minus. We shall keep a Plus activity and discard a Minus.

NOTE.—Of Plus and Minus, some are so obvious that we shall make the change at once. For example,—we shall do all we can at once to secure and keep the right of free association (or government by consent) because we know it is as necessary to us as oxygen: anything new which hinders it for us or others we shall refuse. We shall do all we can at once to have no more war, because common sense tells us it is ruinously wasteful and horribly stupid. Other changes may perhaps be postponed a little: some we shall mark doubtful, and leave for further thought.

Caution. At any time a Plus activity may become a Minus if it is controlled by a group A or B for an A or a B purpose and not for common AB advantage. Example: (i) An Education Act may be a very good Plus; but if it is used by group A to produce a disciplined and obedient proletariat it may be a very dangerous Minus. (ii) The restriction of hours of labour may be a Plus if it prevent unhealthy overwork for any and every worker; but if it is used by men to restrict the hours in which women may work, and made an excuse for keeping women out of trades or processes which they desire to enter, merely for the advantage of men and the disadvantage of women, it becomes a means of keeping women in a position of economic slavery, and is for women a Minus. Also, since a slave population brings down the standard of life for the community which tolerates it, the restriction is a Minus for the whole community. It is not the letter but the spirit which matters most.

The method of classifying the activities of mankind may thus be summarised as follows:

I. Receiving.	Subnormal.	Any of these may be Plus or Minus. Also, any subdivision may overlap into another: there is no clear cleavage-line between them. Also, each may have sub-groups for child and adult; these will overlap too, since it is quite possible for a child to be more evolved than an adult.
	Supranormal.	
II. Harmonising.	Subnormal.	
	Supranormal.	
III. Generating.	Subnormal.	
	Supranormal.	

Examples. Teaching a blinded man to read Braille; Receiving, subnormal, plus. Beating a backward child; Harmonising, subnormal, minus. Wireless telephony; Generating, supranormal, plus. Unemployment doles; Generating, subnormal, minus.

INDIVIDUAL EVOLUTION: ITS AIDS AND HINDRANCES.

It is impossible to give a complete classification here: all that we can do is to indicate the use of the method of inquiry which each individual may employ for himself.

I. *Receiving:* Plus. (*a*) Subnormal. Removal of

THE TENDENCY OF THE INDIVIDUAL 191

adenoids will improve a child's powers of hearing and sight. Rest and holidays will remake its whole nervous system. Remedial exercises, with selected handicrafts, will help a backward child. Typical of this class of aid is a blind man's dog, or a lesson in speech to the 'deaf and dumb.' Here belong school clinics, hospitals, etc. (b) Supra-normal. In this group are all machines which project, multiply or aid sense-reception: telephone, telescope, microscope, microphone, photographic apparatus, telephoto lenses, spectacles, ear-trumpets, stethoscope, the new reflectors which give 'artificial daylight,' slow motion-pictures, submarine signalling, wireless, rulers, gauges, callipers and so on. Games of skill which practise observation, touch, etc., e.g. billiards, tennis, and even spillikins. All practice in appreciation of shape and colour differences, such as is given by drawing, painting, modelling: the feeling for beauty (which predisposes to harmony and therefore to more effective observation) and all the stimuli which produce it, e.g. good furniture, dress, 'the ideal home,' or the costumes, scenery and music of the Russian Ballet. Attempts to combine sense perception in opera. The 'translation' of senses, e.g. the perception of sound through colour, and vice versa. All these are Plus.

Receiving: Minus. This class includes all factors which lessen sense perception. Late hours, poverty, overwork, hunger, sickness, the dread of punishment, too brilliant or too poor lighting, bad ventilation, the fires of furnaces and the like, hand-hardening processes in labour (a harp player is an exception owing to balance of gain), noise in weaving sheds, factories, boilermaking sheds, shipyards, etc., vibrations from motor carriages, so-called 'rainy' or flickering films, the short focus of the eye in streets, street noises.

NOTE.—Under aids to receiving, doubtful, we may group Welfare Work, Works Schools, " Dormitory Towns " such as are proposed in South Wales mining districts; charity organisation societies may be regarded as definitely Minus in their methods. Where these aids are given because of need, and coupled with efforts to secure wages high enough to let the needy buy them for themselves, they may be Plus. If used by group A to maintain or whilst maintaining the subjection of group B, they are Minus.

The majority of forecasts of evolution are concerned mostly with improvements of Receiving and Generating, i.e. I and III, and do nothing (or very little) to increase internal harmony. They aim at a materialist Utopia in which are speed roads and overhead wires, huge balloons, and radio control of machines of enormous size; even destruction is to be on a vast scale. Size would appear to be of great importance to their authors: they suffer from gigantism, and tend to a species of organised megalomania. They are taken up with the efficiency of externals, and the conversion of the East End into a kind of inland Brighton. They do little more than multiply the already crushing mass of stimuli from without which paralyses efforts towards reform.

As I and III are closely connected, we may well consider III immediately, deferring till later the aids to harmony.

III. *Generating :* Plus. (*a*) Subnormal. All educational processes which provide creative work and freedom of experiment (Ch. X and XII). The same factors which aid backward children in I should be included here. (*b*) Supranormal. Both for children and adults this group includes all machines, tools, apparatus, etc., which aid the generation and use of vibrations,—pens for instance, or bicycles. (A bicycle is an excellent example: it multiplies the effect of nerve-cell vibrations which control the movements of the legs, and economises their effort. The bell is an aid to or a substitute for the voice of the rider.) In group III come all multipliers or projectors of vibrations in or produced by the nerve cells controlling movement; megaphones, telephones, telegrams, wireless of all kinds, typewriters, duplicators, the printing press, looms, aeroplanes, trains, motor carriages and tractors, paravanes and the like: gramophones multiply, repeat and give temporary immortality to the voice. The group also includes all instruments of music (obvious aids in generating vibrations): even the 'words and music' of a popular song, sold in the street, belong here.

There is the same tendency here as in group I to combine vibrations (of light, sound, movement, etc.), or to translate the one into the other: a telegram is translated from mouth to hand, to eye, to wire and so on. The complexity of the most ordinary processes of life is well exhibited in the following example. Professor Einstein studies the velocity of light: the English public reads his *Theory of Relativity* (*Popular Exposition*):

the two ends of this process are vibrations in nerve cells in his brain, and vibrations in the brains of all the people who read his book. Einstein presumably 'thinks' not in German but in nerve-cell-vibrations: he translates this into German words, written and (or) spoken. His book is printed, by means of countless brain and machine vibrations and movements: Dr. Lawson receives it in German and translates it into English: it is printed in English, and issued to the English-reading world, who receive it by their senses, harmonise the Professor's original brain vibrations with their own, and—having understood it—proceed to generate further vibrations in their process of acting upon it. Not only is this an example of communication of vibrations,—it is a whole series of examples of varying communities, mental or financial, of employers and employés in the printing, bookbinding and other trades, of publishers, professors and a widely scattered public in a widely extended habitat. It is also a striking example of that community of mental interest which overflows or filters through the artificial boundaries of States.

Generating : Minus. Here belong all hindrances to the generation of vibrations and their resultant activities. Most of the Minus influences in class I are common to class III. With children (especially the subnormal), the compulsions of authority and the dread of punishment are the most potent. Naturally, any conditions tending to lower vitality must be included, such as fatigue, illness, overstrain, bad air, the weather, subnormal physique.

THE TENDENCY OF THE INDIVIDUAL 195

With adults, these are amplified into the whole series of drawbacks to health in modern industrialism : we must add the system of fines, imprisonments, etc., on which the authority of the State depends, and all the repressions which have hindered sublimation of energy. Public opinion, custom, etc., may belong here, e.g. when one hesitates to walk down Bond Street or Piccadilly in the ' wrong ' clothes. The laws, rules or regulations of a defunct community, when used by group A against group B, must also be included. Here too are classed individual controls which arise in II (Harmonising) and become perverted (e.g. fear, hatred), and the influence of propaganda which stops the proper use of the latent period. (As an example of the latter, we may cite the case of the citizen who would normally believe in free association, yet, owing to campaigns in the press and the *ex parte* speeches of politicians, casts his or her vote against the interests of his community (Labour) because of his mistaken conception of the dangers of Communism, or his misinformed fear of freedom for Ireland, etc.) We may now proceed to consider what—evolutionally—is the most important class, No. II, that which includes all processes of Harmonising, and therefore the process of attaining Internal Harmony (Ch. III and XV).

II. *Harmonising :* Plus. (*a*) Subnormal. For children, all educational processes. There is a fascination about the work of helping a backward, slow or muddled child to make links between essential facts, of improving one's own technique of harmony in ' co-operative mentality ' so as to enable him or her to gain greater skill in controlling internal vibrations. This is real education,—not teaching by authority, but helping another to build up his own processes of apperception or imagination, selection or association. The elemental aids of food, rest, sleep, etc., also belong here, and much of what is called After Care. (b) Supra-normal. For children and adults, all that assists in education, study, 'hobbies' even, research: libraries, lectures, concerts, some plays, and steady work (with all the conditions which aid it: it must however be work in harmony with the individual, self-chosen, and creative). Insofar as internal harmony is dependent upon the soul, the 'religious' activities which are best suited to the individual also belong here, e.g. worship, the rosary, etc.

Especially typical of this group should be those activities which aim at establishing harmony in what are called undesirables, unemployables, recidivists, the 'criminal classes' generally. Unfortunately, instead of selecting the harmony of the individual in question as a basis for co-operative mentality, the accepted procedure in prisons is to force the vibrations chosen by authority upon the prisoner, thus further destroying what internal harmony he may have, or—what is equally false—giving him a readymade harmony which is not his own and (when the environment of compulsion is removed) becomes itself discordant and useless.

Harmonising: Minus. Amidst the whirl of stimuli of modern life, the power of selection is one of the most valuable aids to harmony. It is precisely this power which is blunted and debauched by the assertions of authority. Each human being is capable of selection even when an infant: the act is the external symptom of a mutual harmony in vibration (as between mother and child, a pleasing rather than an unpleasing object, etc.). If then we are to develop this power we must do so by using it: selection is evolved by selecting. This implies a chance of error, and therefore a means of 'learning by experience.' But individual experiment except within recognised limits is anathema to authority, which therefore seeks to limit the range of choice, to discourage, to suggest, to 'force a card' upon its subjects. Hence "Don't," or "Because I tell you," for children and adults alike,—or, more subtly (and apparently in accord with free association), the appearance of voluntary choice is maintained. Here belong restrictive legislation, compulsory vaccination and the like: such beliefs as are founded upon punishment and the fear rather than the love of God: many conventional ideas of accepted 'morality,' and much 'expert' advice. Here also belong the publicity campaigns and propaganda of many newspapers, which aim at prejudicing the use of the latent period (Ch. VI, p. 80, note): the reader is so skilfully doped with partial reasoning, the omission of essential facts and even with deliberate misrepresentations that when the occasion arises he can react only in the desired way. A vivid example is the film with a purpose, in which the old faith that 'seeing is believing' is turned to the advantage of a group, and dislike or distrust or amused tolerance of another group or nation cultivated.

In II, *Minus*, must be included all repressions, whether due to the individual himself or to external causes; e.g. fears, secrecies, many so-called 'vices,' suppressed wishes or desires and even the activities in which they find expression.

This incomplete classification may at first seem complicated or unclear, but reference to the summary given in the following chart will show that it is no more than a disentangling of the few simple threads which the loom of life weaves into an involved design. Each individual should continue the process for himself.

Summary of Individual Aids and Hindrances.

By means of such an analysis we may obtain a general view of evolution, of the process of 'becoming' or 'turning out.' It is vitally important to remember that the process goes on now and always; though like the hour-hand of a clock it may not show appreciable movement, yet it still moves, and we can devise means for detecting the movement. It would seem to exhibit two main features, evolution of the more elemental attributes of man, in I and III, and evolution of his internal harmony: in the main the former is swifter than the latter.

In Receiving and Generating, the advance is marked by the raising of individual standards of health, comfort, rest, and efficiency, with a vast increase of the use of machines which should be

SOME AIDS AND HINDRANCES TO INDIVIDUAL VIBRATION.

		PLUS.	MINUS.
I. Receiving	Subnormal	Handicrafts, rest, holidays, school clinics, special exercises, removal of adenoids, teaching dumb to speak, blind to read, blind man's dog, ear-trumpet, slow motion-pictures, spectacles.	Poverty, overwork, late hours, dread of punishment, air raids, noise in street or factory, brilliant light in furnaces, etc., vibrations of motor carriages, processes which harden hands or deafen ears or blind eyes (gas-mantle making), "rainy films," hunger, sickness, dread of losing work.
	Supranormal	Proper lighting, "artificial daylight," country life, "nature study," beauty, telephone, telegraph, microphone, megaphone, microscope, telephoto lens, photography, gauges, rulers, callipers, drawing, painting, modelling.	Works schools. Welfare work. Dormitory towns. Charity.
II. Harmonising	Subnormal	Many school processes. Proper education of "backward" children, development of imagination, and of a sense of rhythm. Control, association, apperception.	Press reports of 'crime.' Acceptance of facts on basis of other's authority. Dread of punishment.
	Supranormal	Libraries. Study. Research. Original work. Proper treatment of 'criminals' and other invalids. Any practice in coexistence on basis of free choice. A general philosophy of life, or 'religion.' Appreciation of art.	Press and film propaganda. Gossip and scandal. Distrust. Lack of self-trust. Threats. Disappointment. Repression, prison, war. Fear of hell. Fear of God, as opposed to love of God.
III. Generating	Subnormal	The same kind of aid as in I, e.g. crutches, chair worked by hand, etc.	Public opinion. "A high standard." Self-distrust, punishment. Also see I.
	Supranormal	Typewriter, gramophone, telephone, wireless, all duplicators, printing press, loom, aeroplane, train, motor carriages. All musical instruments.	See I. Environment of 'civilisation,' overcrowding, poverty, etc.

directed not to the swelling of profits but to the relief of human effort. Against this must be weighed the tendency to obtain evolution by compulsion, which turns Plus into Minus. For example, the compulsory notification of venereal disease is opposed to ultimate evolution because it is compulsory: it is in a line with evolution, however, so to educate young people that before marriage they may think it a decent and honourable thing to do to offer their mate a certificate of health and general fitness.

Individual as well as communal evolution is retarded by the appalling conditions of industrialism which blacken the face of Lancashire and Yorkshire: it is advanced by the use of electric power such as is made in Switzerland or Northern Italy.

Crude and incomplete as the above chart undoubtedly is, it serves to indicate the central danger of modern times to individual (and other) evolution, i.e. the enormous increase in external vibrations without a corresponding increase in internal harmony. It is this which is primarily responsible for the disillusion and disappointment which characterises so many young people to-day, and which—if not remedied—will produce a destructively poisonous cynicism and paralysis of effort. As mental evolution progresses toward increased complexity, sensibility to stimuli, and delicacy of balance, the mind becomes more liable to derangements of every kind. These have their effect even upon the evolving soul,—so that the mind becomes a less efficient instrument of the spirit and the spirit itself becomes disheartened, blunted, and more ready to accept the temporary solace of external things. Internal harmony is after all only the resultant of the forces of soul and body. Those who find comfort in religion may the more easily preserve it, but for many the materialistic and group character of official religion has almost finally discredited it as a vital force. So then it becomes an absolute necessity to revive or make anew the belief of the individual in his destiny: if this cannot be done, he is faced with an internal disorganisation which will cause him to pass from spasmodic intermittent and unconvinced effort into a state of inactivity, which in its turn will merge itself in ultimate decay. We may see the symptoms of such spasmodic effort in the post-war dashing from extreme to extreme of selfishness or altruism, of self-indulgence and social service, the almost frenzied attempts to find satisfaction in pleasure, or wealth, or overwork, or fresh interests and occupations. Such exaggerations are symptoms of a loss of a central sense of proportion, and thus of an incipient madness, which leads to every kind of nervous breakdown. The whole effort of post-war reconstruction should be aimed at the perfection of internal harmony, whether of the individual or the community, and the removal of possible causes of its disturbance. But it must also be remembered that, though the war has exaggerated its symptoms, the lag of internal behind external evolution has characterised human progress for centuries: it is a disease of long standing, and is not to be removed by treating its symptoms. Nothing but a determined attack on first causes will rid us of it for ever.

CHAPTER XVII

THE TENDENCY OF THE COMMUNITY

BEFORE considering the tendency of community we shall do well to examine some immediate results of war, both Minus and Plus, which are not markedly individual or communal, but partake of the nature of both. They resemble external complications of an illness which if disregarded may render recovery doubtful or even impossible, e.g. the unsatisfactory home environment which retards a patient's progress and renders a 'change of air' imperative.

SOME POST-WAR AIDS AND HINDRANCES.

One result of the past struggle was a breaking down of social barriers: there had been an emotional tendency to regard all men and women as equal in suffering and sacrifice, with a revival (of course strictly within the limits of empire and alliances) of the doctrine of the brotherhood of man. It is not too much to say that a majority of the individuals on each side felt themselves members of a body: to that extent they became a community. It needed only a turn of the mind to expand this into a real relationship which would have included friend and enemy. But this never occurred more than sporadically: indeed it would have been fatal to the continued existence of the international group A. Fortunately for the group such an expansion was rendered impossible by an intensive propaganda and a revival of the mistaken theory that the State is a community. But the temporary feeling of solidarity has left its mark on post-war mentality, and human beings have now an increased bias towards the theory of equality: they are less ready to tolerate privilege or to accept servitude, and more inclined to criticise the disadvantages of their environment. A genuine statesmanship would seize on this as an aid to remodelling the organisation of the State: group A sees in it merely another menace to stability, and meets it with the threat of compulsion. The group A remedy for group B is not more leisure but more work: thus a condition which might have been made Plus becomes Minus. Yet however successful A may prove in suppressing B, the chief result is to drive inwards a general discontent, so that the individual members of B harbour a strong and increasing personal resentment which destroys their internal harmony.

It is impossible to disregard the widespread atmosphere of distrust which at present vitiates human coexistence: it is a natural but lamentable result of a prolonged and concentrated effort of hate of an enemy. A people which for years has been goaded and coaxed and bullied into exhibitions of mingled dread and hatred is left after the crisis in a condition of collapse, with neither the energy to rouse itself from lethargy nor the will to break the habit it has contracted. It is like a drug-taker deprived of his drug, craving and never satiated. The habit of distrust extends to friend as well as enemy, and to-day the natural instinctive basis of human intercourse—viz. mutual trust—is disregarded or despised. Worse still, those who gave the stimulant have themselves lost the power of trust: they have made themselves incapable of realising when others speak the truth and this moral failure vitiates their whole scheme of international relations. It is an appalling example of the deliberate destruction of collective harmony, the effects of which have penetrated the very being of its authors, destroying their individual harmony and rendering them incapable of organising human coexistence. It is a recurring Minus.

There is one post-war hindrance which is above all others Minus in its effects upon evolution. Among the hindrances to individuals we classified poverty, hunger, sickness and the like, with mental derangement which had its effect even upon the soul, so that spirit itself became disheartened, blunted and discordant. Symptoms of such disorders are common amongst individuals in this island, and will act as centres of infection for years to come. These are however relatively unimportant when compared with the mass-disturbance of mentality among the peoples of Central Europe. Defeat may be forgotten, may even be a Plus: disease may be isolated and overcome: hunger may be relieved. But defeat plus hunger plus disease plus poverty form a breeding ground

THE TENDENCY OF THE COMMUNITY 205

for an insanity which even adult minds cannot hope to escape. When such conditions form the heredity and the environment of infancy, childhood and youth, the result may be enough to divert the course of evolution so that whole nations may 'turn out' Minus. Our study of life compels us to admit the pressing need of co-operation not only among individuals and communities but amongst States as well, if mankind is to continue to live on this earth. A reasoned policy based upon a knowledge of life would concentrate every effort upon improving the environment of millions of subnormal beings. We observe on the contrary an organised effort on the part of groups in neighbouring States to perpetuate the very environment which has produced the disease, and so to reduce the vitality of individuals in the infected area that for a century at least they may not regain a normal health.[1] Indeed, one of these states has gone so far in internal discord that she has drawn upon the black inhabitants of her colonies to continue the repression of which her own depleted energy is incapable,—an appalling symptom of an epidemic insanity such as the world has rarely seen. Were it an isolated case the future would be dark enough: when the allies of the state in question look on without protest at such an outrage of the decencies of life, hope would seem to be wellnigh gone.

Such being the actual relations between modern

[1] Cf. the newspaper campaign of a part of group A in England against the relief of starving Russian children, November–December 1921.

States, the ordinary man and woman may be excused if they refuse to regard the State as the highest form of human community.

But if the internal harmony of the individual is behindhand in evolution, and the atmosphere in which he lives is one of distrust and disillusion, what can we expect of the communities of which he is a member? Let us examine a sample community, under the three heads of Receiving, Harmonising and Generating vibrations.

A Specimen of Community.

Suppose two individuals to unite in a commercial enterprise. *Receiving*, each enjoys the assistance of the other. *Harmonising*, they draw up an agreement to direct their common activities. *Generating*, they proceed about the business for which they have combined. Suppose them now successful: they wish to extend the business and are in need of capital, so they decide to float a company. *Receiving*, the shares are issued and the capital subscribed. *Harmonising*, they allocate the capital as need demands: they appoint directors, manager, etc. *Generating* is represented by the further conduct of the business. The shareholders are in ' voluntary association ': the relation of employers and employed is one of common purpose or advantage. Here however enters a new factor, the desire for maximum profit: the business is no longer primarily intended to supply the needs of the consumer and to secure no more than a reasonable margin to the producer: it has

THE TENDENCY OF THE COMMUNITY 207

become a 'business transaction' with a special code of morality of its own: it is an affair of maximum profit. From this follows an irreducible minimum expense on production (which includes wages), with the inevitable separation of community into groups A and B. Internal harmony being weak, and distrust permeating all human relationships, we may expect—and indeed we find—B dissatisfied and A resorting to compulsion by economic or other means. B responds by strikes or sabotage, A appeals to authority, law and force. Both then exhibit clearly a diseased condition. [Here belong Trusts, Combines, Mergers and the like.]

Ultimately the flaw is discovered to be an internal individual discord, and though something may be done by councils, trade-boards and arbitration we can but alleviate symptoms. The central source of the disease can only be treated in the individual, and thus the one means to a radical cure is to bring up children whose internal harmony is proof against disturbance from without. The cure cannot be effected in our time, but only in the future: in the present all that we can do is to employ makeshift first aid, though by common sense and methodical study we make reasonably certain that our first-aid measures are Plus and not Minus. (Example. The Company we have imagined goes bankrupt and the employés are out of work. First-aid measures will aim at relief of unemployment. Doles will be rejected as obviously Minus, since we know them to be a drug or poison to human effort and not a tonic or a food. State aid will provide " work of individual importance," i.e. creative work, with such a wage that the man or woman who does the work shall feel free and independent and be conscious of doing something at once stimulating to self and valuable to others. It is surely not beyond the wit of man to organise a peace.)

GENERAL CONDITIONS AFFECTING COMMUNITY.

(i) It cannot be too often repeated that a community is as yet neither a State nor a Nation. A community is an association of two or more human beings for common (though not of necessity identical or similar) purpose or advantage in their evolution. A State, both now and for a period at least including the known history of mankind, is an organisation for securing group purpose or advantage. (This is equally true of states whether governed by an " upper class " or by a " class-conscious proletariat," by a conquering nation or by a native group. The tendency of community in Ireland will show this to be the relation of ' Capital ' and ' Labour ' even in the face of foreign invasion.) A " Nation," if it means anything more than a past stage of human evolution, denotes a comparatively unmixed stock in a position of relative (geographic) isolation, such as may be seen to-day in the case of the Esquimaux or the people of Tierra del Fuego. The development of communications, of transport and trade have long since broken down such barriers in Europe and America. Nations to-day are economic organisations and no longer racial units, and since economic organisations tend more and more to be controlled by groups they cannot be regarded as communities. A Community is essentially a natural life-form or organism: a State has never yet been more than an artificial organisation.

(ii) The vitality of a community may be estimated by the internal harmony which it possesses: this harmony of a community is the common chord of the individual harmonies of its members. (And since the internal harmony of the individual is disturbed by modern conditions, we may expect to find the vitality of many communities to be extremely low. A case in point is the 'Triple Alliance' in England, 1921.)

(iii) The value of a community may be assessed by the amount of advantage it secures to its individual members. Examples: a Co-operative Society, or an Employers' Federation.

(iv) In a community, whatever is evolutionally Minus for an individual is so for the community: what is Plus for him or her is Plus for it. (It follows that those conditions which in industrial 'civilisation' are harmful to the individual are harmful to the community, and that such 'civilisation' may be an obstacle to human development.)

(v) It is by no means essential that a community should be everlasting. Though on occasions it may be adapted to serve a new common purpose, or be maintained by its members for reasons of sentiment long after its usefulness has ended, it is always a life-form subject to change, and liable to be discarded by those who made it as soon as they discover a more advantageous method of coexistence.

Two Further Examples of Community.

There are as many communities as there are human activities, varying enormously in potential energy and in evolutionary value. It is impossible to give examples of every species: we may however obtain a general idea of their range by examining two which seem to be at opposite ends of the scale.

(i) Outside the ring fence of a sleek well-timbered park four human beings sat in a dry ditch. The father nursed one small child, the mother watched a second as it began to crawl out on to the dusty road. Beside them stood a 'pram' in which all their worldly goods were packed. Last night was the first time for two days that they had tasted bread: they had no money left, and neither man nor woman had had work for six months. Yes, it was the same almost all over the world, the man growled out: it came of serving your king and country. The children were all right: the weather had been good for them. The woman hoped there might be work in the next town, or in the fields or hop-gardens.

Surely this is near the low-water mark of life. " Receiving " has almost ceased as a function of this community: " generating " is sinking below the zero line of observation: " harmonising " becomes more and more impossible as bodily and spiritual energies fade into the apathy of silence.

THE TENDENCY OF THE COMMUNITY 211

(ii) In every country, undivided by the frontiers of States, a new community is slowly taking form: its chief characteristic is the more evolved internal harmony of its members: the vibrations which it generates are tuned to a common chord of belief and hope. It is scattered widely through this and other lands, loosely but effectively linked by a mental and spiritual enthusiasm which transcends all creeds. Its members are by no means all of one Church: most of them would never think of themselves as good. Broadly speaking they are those who by theory or practice have learnt the true function of government, and realised the need of internal harmony. They include in their community many women and some men, and even children. Their occupations range from the top to the bottom of the social scale: a few are employers, more are employés, some are teachers of adults and some of children. Relying for their purpose entirely upon the 'natural controls,' and seeking common rather than individual advantage, they had a widespread influence on opposing States even during the recent war: they are gradually gaining an international significance. In case of need they can find a friend to help another's friend almost anywhere. *Though almost invariably interested in some much-needed reform, they are not to be specially sought in important official positions, nor have they an influential committee, or large premises or wealthy funds, or even any definite organisation.* By reason of their constant effort to attain internal harmony, they are able to generate vibrations which are restoring to the world that trust and mutual confidence which it has been the purpose of governments to destroy: they are re-creating life and energy in weakened bodies and wounded souls all over Europe to-day. Whatever theory or belief inspires them, their practice is in direct accord with human need, and in the harmony they create may be found the greatest if not indeed the only promise of hope for the future of mankind.

Community : Summary.

It is unfortunate that words should change their meaning: it is even more so that they should gather up other meanings from time to time, barnacles of thought that hide the form of the original. When to these natural processes are added the deliberate or the sincere errors of those who use them, it becomes almost impossible to arrive at a clear and simple expression of an idea. Having as children learnt that school is a community, having as adults been taught that the State is a community, we have first of all to divest our minds of the meanings associated in them with the word, and then begin afresh to study its real meaning, or rather the real meaning of the phenomena which it describes. We are not so much concerned with origin and derivation as with examining a fact of life: it is not the label on the bottle so much as the contents which we have to consider.

Two men on one road, each driving a car and

THE TENDENCY OF THE COMMUNITY

having to pass the other, exhibit all the essentials of community. They coexist, they co-operate, and having attained their common purpose they separate and proceed to other combination: they harmonise their movements according to a rule of the road which neither would hesitate to break in case of need. Their common action is a lifeform conditioned by their environment: when it has served its purpose it ends, though the serving of the purpose remains as an incident in their course and contributes to their future.

Community is an organism, State is an organisation. We observe then the known world inhabited by human beings in constant movement and co-operation for varying purposes, using community as a labour-saving device, a means of economising and multiplying effort, and gradually evolving a technique of coexistence based upon experience and known to everyone as common sense. An indispensable factor of this technique is recognition of the needs and claims of others. This then is human coexistence, and so successful has it been that it has secured to the individual an overplus of opportunity for the reception and generation of vibrations. So to say, the interest on his capital has accumulated faster than the growth of his power to use it: in other words, his internal harmony has lagged behind, and owing to the vibrations of unselected stimuli from without has become discordant. One of the first results of such discord is the failure to recognise the needs of others: from this individual want proceeds the disintegration of community, its separation into

A and B, and the consequent repression of one group by another. It is at this stage of evolution that formal government begins, and manifests itself in what we know as States.

These experimental organisations have invariably been controlled by the group which desired the permanence of a divided community, and opposed by that group which wished for change. Whatever the form of government has been, tribal, autocratic, oligarchic or other, men have remained convinced that the right of voluntary association is essential to their freedom and evolution. This conviction inspired the two great pronouncements of Democracy made almost simultaneously[1] by a Latin and a Teutonic State. "We hold these truths to be self-evident, that all men are created equal, that they are endowed by their Creator with certain inalienable Rights, that amongst these are Life, Liberty, and the pursuit of Happiness, that to secure these rights, Governments are instituted, deriving their just powers from the consent of the governed." (American Declaration of Independence.) "Men are born and continue equal in respect of their rights. The end of political society is the preservation of the natural and imprescriptible rights of man. These rights are liberty, property, security, and resistance to oppression. The principle of all Sovereignty resides essentially in the nation. No body, nor individual, can exert any authority which is not expressly derived from it." (Declaration of the Rights of Man,

[1] America 1776, France 1791. If we remember the length of world-history, the difference of fifteen years is negligible.

THE TENDENCY OF THE COMMUNITY

made by the National Assembly of France.) Those who wish to study in detail the history of these experiments should consult Bryce's comprehensive survey of democracy.[1]

If, after almost one hundred and fifty years, we find the Federal troops at war with the miners of Virginia, and France sick in mind and spirit with the delirium of power, we may well examine the documents of their incorporation for the flaw which has brought their citizens not Liberty but slavery, not Security but terror, not Life but death. Perhaps a later age may realise that governments are of themselves unable to secure either liberty or happiness, that resistance to oppression is a delusion, and may focus the internal harmony of countless communities not upon man's rights but on his needs.

Modern Democracies, Bryce. Macmillan, 1921.

CHAPTER XVIII

PLUS OR MINUS ?

THOUGH evolution seems infinitely slow, though nothing happens in it without due cause, there are occasions when its effects take shape with apparently explosive quickness. The flash of lightning, the avalanche, the tidal wave, all have their gradual growth, which may be observed and studied: the volcano gives warning of the change of form which its imprisoned energy is about to make: the frozen river lifts and cracks the ice which binds it. Human activities too exhibit the same phenomena: from time to time we feel that something is about to happen (something—that is—striking enough to be appreciated by our limited senses, for in reality everything is happening always). It would seem as though such a time had come, and that the children of to-day would see during their lifetime a new form of government evolved, the internationalisation of group A for the world-control of B.

In almost every corner of the earth there is unrest and discontent,—group B seeking change, group A opposing it. Within the frontiers of States group A has already taken shape as Coalition,— a pooling of group interests and resources against dissolution, a concentration of effort against reform. Its next stage has begun. The new day shows the Entente, sprung up like a fungus, and its shadow, the League of Nations, lying behind it. Quite soon now, when group A in ' enemy ' countries has fastened its hold once more upon the State, we shall see a swift cohering of interest and power all over the world, under some name which will once more convince group B that the freedom of action of B is unimpaired. There will follow an era of world-control by international force, the financial-governing group in all lands forming a community with the common purpose of resisting change. And since this purpose is opposed to life the effect upon human evolution will be Minus.

The process is well seen in the following quotations from the correspondence between the representatives of an Entente State and of one which desires to remain outside it.

(1) " The common concern of Great Britain and Ireland by land and sea shall be mutually recognised. . . . The position of Ireland is also of great importance for the Air Services. . . ."
(2) " No common action can be secured by force." (British proposals for settlement, July 20, 1921.)
(3) " True friendship with England . . . can be obtained most readily now through amicable but absolute separation." (Irish reply, August 10, 1921.)
(4) " Nothing is to be gained by prolonging a theoretical discussion." (British reply, August 13, 1921.)

In (1) we see how modern policy is unable to escape from the ancient three-phase structure of earth-material : (2) is an admission of man's need of liberty : (3) is an assertion of that liberty, which will not be met by substituting a Governor-General for a Lord-Lieutenant : (4) is the rejection of the laws of coexistence by a group which wishes to perpetuate a defunct community : it is the kind of statement which almost makes one despair of humanity.

What have we to set in the scales against group A ? Nothing but the internal harmony of the individual, the kernel from which all growth must spring. It is the centre from which all progress radiates. Itself it can neither be seen nor handled : its results alone are visible. From it, and through its natural controls, there comes that unhindered flow and change of coexistence which is life. On its improvement depends the future of mankind.

Yet though we remain bound another hundred or a thousand years, though we have not yet seen the last of destruction and wars and the age-old disease of slavery, we should remember that human evolution is no longer physical but mental and spiritual. We no longer have to do with the infinitely dragging development of hand or wing,[1] with bone or muscle.[2] Man has a mind able to conceive abstractions, to grasp at truth : he has a soul by which to draw upon the eternal forces of the infinite. Given the will to freedom he may be free, not by force or repression, but by the natural controls which have guided him through the ages.

We may not be able to rid ourselves at once of

---

[1] *Beginnings of Flight*, Lucas.
[2] *Der Bau des Menschen*, Wiedersheim.

the past forms which hinder our present movement, but we can always see that the temporary alterations we make shall be in accord with the principles of life and thus at least not future obstacles. In this we may be guided by a truer conception of government.

'*The proper function of government is the securing of individual freedom.*' Not, that is, the greatest good of the greatest number; this implies less good for some and is a cause of group antagonism. What is required is proportionate good for all, and—since needs differ—this will generally mean a different good for each.

We need not try to make a complete list of the special applications of the principle of freedom: each individual must make his own, guided by natural control. Such a list might include freedom of trade and transport, the opening of the Dardanelles and the Suez and Panama Canals, of great railways and roads and airways, the dismantling of fortifications and the abolition of frontiers, the installation of private wireless in every home, the end of ugliness and the beginning of beauty. Yet all these and more would but be the symptoms of freedom of internal harmony, the phenomena of an inward reality. It is an old lesson, but one that we have still to learn, that all reform is from within.

It is not by state, or government, or organisation or armament that the world will be made safe for humanity, but by individual effort towards internal harmony. Every effort is of value: every child brought up by natural control and not by external authority is a bulwark against the domination of a group, a living force which in the daily experience of community will achieve a Plus of evolution. We have no need to give up hope, to sink under discontent or disillusion. Having made the world what it is and ourselves what we are, we may set ourselves with cheerful faith and a sane common sense to help others to make co-existence what we know it ought to be.

BIBLIOGRAPHY

BAYERLEIN. Jena oder Sedan? Vita Deutsches Verlagshaus. Berlin, 1903.
BAYLISS. Principles of General Physiology. Longmans, Green. 1920.
BOWEN, M. I Will Maintain. The Viper of Milan.
BRYCE (Lord). Modern Democracies. Macmillan. 1921.
CHAMBERLIN AND SALISBURY. Geology. 3 vols. John Murray. 1905.
CHAMBERLIN. The Origin of the Earth. University of Chicago Press.
DOSTOIEFFSKY. House of the Dead. (Everyman's Library.) Dent.
EBERLEIN. Schwarze am Rhein. Schroeder. Heidelberg. 1921.
GORING, C. The English Convict. H.M. Stationery Office. 1913.
HALLIBURTON. Handbook of Physiology. John Murray. 1907.
HAKLUYT. Principal Navigations. Glasgow, 1904.
KIPLING. The Day's Work. Macmillan.
KROPOTKIN. Mutual Aid. Heinemann. 1915.
LONDON, J. The Iron Heel.
LOW, B. Psychoanalysis. Brief Account of Freudian Theory. George Allen & Unwin. 1921.
LUCAS, F. A. Beginnings of Flight. *American Museum Journal*, vol. xvi, 1916.
LULL, R. S. Organic Evolution. New York. Macmillan. 1917.
MCDOUGALL. The Group Mind. Cambridge University Press. 1920.

BIBLIOGRAPHY

MERRIMAN, S. The Vultures.

Military Medical Manuals. University of London Press. 1918, etc.

MONTESSORI. Montessori Method (translation). Heinemann. 1912.

NATIONAL ASSOCIATION FOR THE ADVANCEMENT OF THE COLORED PEOPLE. Thirty Years of Lynching in the U.S. 1889–1918. New York, 1920.

OSBORN, H. F. The Law of Adaptive Radiation. *American Naturalist*, vol. xxxvi.

PARKMAN. The Jesuits in North America. Macmillan. 1912.

PERRIN. Brownian Movement and Molecular Reality. (Translated by Soddy.) Taylor & Francis. 1910.

PRESCOTT. Conquest of Mexico. Swan Sonnenschein.

Report of Commission on the Rising in the Punjab. H.M. Stationery Office.

SANDBURG. Chicago Race Riots. Harcourt Brace & Howe. New York, 1920.

SOUTHARD, E. E. Shell Shock and other Neuropsychiatric Problems. W. M. Leonard. Boston, 1919.

STARR. Organic and Functional Nervous Diseases. Baillière, Tindall & Cox. 1910.

STODDART. Mind and its Disorders.

SUDERMANN. Die Ehre. Cotta'sche Buchhandlung. Stuttgart and Berlin, 1903.

WIEDERSHEIM, R. Der Bau des Menschen. 1902.

WILLSON. The Great Company. Smith, Elder. 1900.

WATSON. Evolution. Jack. 1915.

INDEX

Adolescence, 44
Amœba, 33
Ants, 92, 94, 95
Association, paths, 35, 38; voluntary, 120
Atmosphere, 23, 24, 27; ultra-, 27, 28, 37, 40
Attention, 39, 59; definition, 66, 80
Authority, 45, 47, 136, 140; definition, 65, 78; diseases, 170–179; of A over B, 109; paternal, 97; reactions of B, 177

Bees, 92
Brain, 36, 102; definition, 65
Brownian movement, 19, 37, 47

Cell, constituents, 85; division, 87; membrane, 30; single, 30, 33; staining, 31, 32; vibration, 88
Cells, 38; specialised, 89
Charcot's bell-concept, 37
Childhood, strains, 46, 47
Child life, 134
Coalition, 216
Co-existence, 9; cells, 89; dual, 106; evolution, 60; formula, 107; uses of formula, 108; natural controls, 115, 169; study, 102; technique, 116, 136
Colour line, 152–155, 205
Common sense, 8, 116, 117, 123, 157, 187; as neurasthenia, 167
Community, 37, 49; body, 88; cessation, 109, 152, 171, 209; classification, 103; comparison, 101; compulsion, 171, 177; conditions, 208; definition, 65, 78; disease, 160; dissolution and regrouping, 50, 89, 127, 155–163; division, 87; human and other, 85, 96, 129; individual and, 86; insect and animal, 90–96; lesson, 135; mental, 128, 129, 139, 164; Red Indians, 96; sanctity, 125, 126, 130; school, 131; soul, 105; specimen, 206, 210, 211; three phases, 105; various, of the individual, 123–130
Compulsion, mechanism, 172, 177
Contact-horizons, 25, 26, 30, 135
Co-operation, children, 9, 128
Co-operative mentality, 136, 137, 169

Death, 34, 89; definition, 64
Definitions, need, 57; list, 64; notes, 67
Discipline, 168; definition, 65, 78
Discord, 43, 44, 45, 47, 48, 139; group, 148, 150; individual, 207; of B, 174
Disease, definition, 66; in States, 147–157, causes and symptoms, 158

Earth, growth, 23
Education, definition, 66; group, 165, 168
Electric fish, 40
Environment, human, 93; relation to, 128; vertical and horizontal, 92
Evolution, 25, 50; aids and hindrances, 190; conditions, 186; compulsion, 200; definition, 64; Downs, 60; man's present stage, 156, 185; mental, 128, 200, 218; method of study, 188

Fear, 133; mechanism, 175
Frontiers, 6, 166, 219

God, belief in, 62
Government by consent, 171; example, 147; function, 219
Gravity, 27, 40
Growth, 47; definition, 65, 77

Habit, 35, 38; definition, 65, 79
Habitat, man, 26; life, 92

INDEX

Harmony, 44, 45, 46; internal (community), 136, 138, 172; (individual), 47, 48, 50, 52, 178, 196, 218, 219; modern disturbances, 200, 201
Human being, definition, 64, 67
Hydrosphere, 23, 24

Individual, advantage, 10; and his communities, 123–130; sacrifice of, 78, 125; tendency of evolution, 185–201
Intelligentsia, 130, 150, 163
Ireland, 110, 208, 217

Latent period, 50; definition, 66, 80; misuse, 53, 195, 197; use, 117
Law, 171; definition, 66, 79
League of Nations, 60, 100, 217
Liberty, relative, 89
Life, definition, 64, 71; origin, 24, 25
Lithosphere, 23, 24

Memory, 39; definition, 65, 75
Mentality, mass-disturbance, 204
Microscope, 31, 32, 33
Molecules, 20, 26, 27, 37, 40
Montessori, 138
Movement, amœba, 33, 34; characteristic of man, 21, 28, 29, 34, 35, 36; communities, 61; life, 34; protoplasm, 30, 33, 34; reflex, 33; senses, 35; thought, 36, 37
Movement-community, 124, 140, 213

Nation, 208
Nerves, brain, 36; gemmules, 34
Nervous system, 50; definition, 64, 73
Nucleus, 85; division, 87

Obedience, 141; definition, 65, 79
Over-stimulation, 45, 46
Over-strain, 47
Ownership of land, 100

Penguin, 26
Personality, change, 38, 39, 177; definition, 65, 76; extension, 43

Phases of matter, 20, 21, 22, 23, 24, 25, 61, 217
Planetesimal hypothesis, 22, 24
Politeness, 52
Protoplasm, 30, 32, 33; vibration, 34

Religion, 61, 98, 99
Repression, 138, 168, 177, 198
Reproduction by division, 33, 87, 104
Resolution of discord, 44, 45, 48

School, community, 131; life, 45; lines of cleavage, 132, 138; social system, 132
Self-reliance, 118
Senses, 28, 29; movement, 35; perception, 37; translation, 191
Soul, community, 105, 106; definition, 64, 67
Specialisation, 88, 95, 96
Spiral nebula, 22
State, 148; diseases, 149
Stimulus, 27, 39, 40, 46; definition, 64, 72
Sympathy, 117

Tact, 118
Ticket-community, 125

Vibration, aids, 119; cell, 33, 34, 36, 37, 44; characteristic of man, 21, 28, 29; communities, 61, 89; discordant, 42; water, air, 24, 28, 35; generation, 40, 41, 48; harmonising, 42, 43, 44, 46, 104, 125, 196; increased complexity, 49; individual, 104; limits, 26, 27; translation, 191; transmission, 41
Violin, 90
Voluntary association, 120, 157, 206, 214

White Army, 151, 157
Women, disadvantage, 190; under payment, 163
Words, meaning, 8
Work, creative, 5, 119, 160, 208

For Product Safety Concerns and Information please contact our EU representative GPSR@taylorandfrancis.com
Taylor & Francis Verlag GmbH, Kaufingerstraße 24, 80331 München, Germany